Women's Rights

Other Books of Related Interest

Women's Rights

Shasta Gaughen, *Book Editor*

Daniel Leone, *President*
Bonnie Szumski, *Publisher*
Scott Barbour, *Managing Editor*
Brenda Stalcup, *Series Editor*

Contemporary Issues
Companion

GREENHAVEN
PRESS ®

THOMSON

™

GALE

San Diego • Detroit • New York • San Francisco • Cleveland
New Haven, Conn. • Waterville, Maine • London • Munich

THOMSON
★
GALE

LIBRARY OF CONGRESS CATALOGING-IN-PUBLICATION DATA

Women's rights / Shasta Gaughen, book editor.
   p. cm. — (Contemporary issues companion)
Includes bibliographical references and index.
ISBN 0-7377-0848-4 (pbk. : alk. paper) — ISBN 0-7377-0849-2 (hb : alk. paper)
   1. Women's rights. I. Gaughen, Shasta. II. Series.
HQ1236 .W65265 2003
305.42—dc21   2002072226

Printed in the United States of America

CONTENTS

FOREWORD

In the news, on the streets, and in neighborhoods, individuals are confronted with a variety of social problems. Such problems may affect people directly: A young woman may struggle with depression, suspect a friend of having bulimia, or watch a loved one battle cancer. And even the issues that do not directly affect her private life—such as religious cults, domestic violence, or legalized gambling—still impact the larger society in which she lives. Discovering and analyzing the complexities of issues that encompass communal and societal realms as well as the world of personal experience is a valuable educational goal in the modern world.

Effectively addressing social problems requires familiarity with a constantly changing stream of data. Becoming well informed about today's controversies is an intricate process that often involves reading myriad primary and secondary sources, analyzing political debates, weighing various experts' opinions—even listening to first-hand accounts of those directly affected by the issue. For students and general observers, this can be a daunting task because of the sheer volume of information available in books, periodicals, on the evening news, and on the Internet. Researching the consequences of legalized gambling, for example, might entail sifting through congressional testimony on gambling's societal effects, examining private studies on Indian gaming, perusing numerous websites devoted to Internet betting, and reading essays written by lottery winners as well as interviews with recovering compulsive gamblers. Obtaining valuable information can be time-consuming—since it often requires researchers to pore over numerous documents and commentaries before discovering a source relevant to their particular investigation.

Greenhaven's Contemporary Issues Companion series seeks to assist this process of research by providing readers with useful and pertinent information about today's complex issues. Each volume in this anthology series focuses on a topic of current interest, presenting informative and thought-provoking selections written from a wide variety of viewpoints. The readings selected by the editors include such diverse sources as personal accounts and case studies, pertinent factual and statistical articles, and relevant commentaries and overviews. This diversity of sources and views, found in every Contemporary Issues Companion, offers readers a broad perspective in one convenient volume.

In addition, each title in the Contemporary Issues Companion series is designed especially for young adults. The selections included in every volume are chosen for their accessibility and are expertly edited in consideration of both the reading and comprehension levels of the audience. The structure of the anthologies also enhances accessibility. An introductory essay places each issue in context and provides helpful facts such as historical background or current statistics and legislation that pertain to the topic. The chapters that follow organize the material and focus on specific aspects of the book's topic. Every essay is introduced by a brief summary of its main points and biographical information about the author. These summaries aid in comprehension and can also serve to direct readers to material of immediate interest and need. Finally, a comprehensive index allows readers to efficiently scan and locate content.

The Contemporary Issues Companion series is an ideal launching point for research on a particular topic. Each anthology in the series is composed of readings taken from an extensive gamut of resources, including periodicals, newspapers, books, government documents, the publications of private and public organizations, and Internet websites. In these volumes, readers will find factual support suitable for use in reports, debates, speeches, and research papers. The anthologies also facilitate further research, featuring a book and periodical bibliography and a list of organizations to contact for additional information.

A perfect resource for both students and the general reader, Greenhaven's Contemporary Issues Companion series is sure to be a valued source of current, readable information on social problems that interest young adults. It is the editors' hope that readers will find the Contemporary Issues Companion series useful as a starting point to formulate their own opinions about and answers to the complex issues of the present day.

INTRODUCTION

In August 1920, the Nineteenth Amendment was ratified, guaranteeing American women the right to vote. Thus ended a decades-long struggle by suffrage activists to ensure that women were allowed the same right as men to participate in the electoral process. The long fight for suffrage that culminated in the ratification of the Nineteenth Amendment is known as the "first wave" of American feminism.

The first feminists were concerned with other issues besides the right to vote. In speeches and publications, at rallies and conventions, they addressed women's unequal status in education, the law, politics, and the home. In 1860, Elizabeth Cady Stanton argued that women were entitled to the same rights as men, stating that "the natural rights of the civilized man and woman are government, property, the harmonious development of all their powers, and the gratification of their desires." Although Susan B. Anthony is primarily remembered for her work within the suffrage movement, she also strove to secure women's equality in other areas. In an 1875 speech, for instance, she maintained that "girls, like boys, must be educated to some lucrative employment; women, like men, must have equal chances to earn a living." But winning women's suffrage was the predominant goal of feminism's first wave, and after the passage of the Nineteenth Amendment, the women's rights movement entered a period of decline.

Through the 1950s, the main role for women in the United States was that of housewife and mother. Women were encouraged to focus their talents and energy on keeping a proper home, raising and nurturing their children, supporting their husband's career goals, and acting as a gracious and accomplished hostess. While some women did attend college and most held jobs before marriage, these experiences were meant to contribute to their eventual goal of becoming a well-rounded wife and mother. By the early 1960s, however, it was becoming apparent that many women were dissatisfied with the limitations of their prescribed role.

In 1963, journalist Betty Friedan publicized this growing discontent in a book called *The Feminine Mystique*. For years, Friedan argued, women had been trained to believe that ultimate fulfillment would come from being wives and mothers. They "were taught to pity the neurotic, unfeminine, unhappy women who wanted to be poets or physicists or presidents," she wrote. "They learned that truly feminine women do not want careers, higher education, political rights—the independence and the opportunities that the old-fashioned feminists fought for." In reality, Friedan insisted, many women felt trapped and unfulfilled in the housewife role, longing to achieve something more in life. *The Feminine Mystique* was an overnight sensation and is popularly considered to have sparked the "second wave" of feminism.

The second wave, often called the women's liberation movement, quickly expanded to address a myriad of issues. Women did not just want to escape the boredom of being a homemaker; they wanted equality in all aspects of American life. Middle-class housewives were eager to expand their horizons, returning to college and embarking on careers in fields such as politics, medicine, and law. Young female students worked to eradicate stereotypes that defined them solely as sexual objects at the same time that they pushed for new freedoms in sexual behavior and reproductive choices. Working women desired fair and equal wages, protection from job discrimination, and child care. As more women became permanent members of the working world during the 1960s and 1970s, they increasingly drew attention to gender inequities in wages, working conditions, and career options. The National Organization for Women (NOW), founded in 1966, was initially dedicated to the promotion of equality in the workplace.

The women's liberation movement was closely linked to the civil rights movement. Many feminists drew parallels between the struggles of black Americans for equality and their own campaign for women's rights. One important victory was Title VII of the 1964 Civil Rights Act, which prohibited employment discrimination based on race; it was amended to include a provision that made sex discrimination in employment against the law. Ironically, the language including sex discrimination was added to the amendment with the intention of preventing it from passing. This attempt failed, and Title VII eventually became a powerful tool in fighting workplace discrimination based on race or gender.

The feminists of the second wave also championed a cause originally promoted by the women of the first wave: the Equal Rights Amendment (ERA). After the passage of the Nineteenth Amendment, leading suffragist Alice Paul authored the ERA, which she intended to provide constitutional protection for equal rights for women. The amendment was introduced in each session of Congress from 1923 through the 1960s, but it received little public backing until the revitalization of the women's movement. In 1967, NOW threw its support behind the ERA. In 1971, the amendment passed the House of Representatives. In 1972, the Senate approved the amendment as well, setting a time limit of seven years for ratification by at least two-thirds of the fifty states.

The fight for ratification created great controversy. Although many organizations, including the League of Women Voters and the American Federation of Labor and Congress of Industrial Organizations (AFL-CIO), supported the ERA, there was much political opposition to the amendment. By 1977, thirty-five of the necessary thirty-eight states had ratified the ERA, but time was growing short, and in 1978 the deadline for ratification was extended to 1982. The final deadline of June 1982 arrived with the ERA still three states short of ratification. Since then, the ERA has been reintroduced to Congress every year but has never been put to a vote.

Patricia Ireland, former president of NOW, is one of many contemporary feminists who maintain that passage of the ERA is still necessary. "Women are still paid less on the job and charged more for everything from dry cleaning to insurance," Ireland argues. "The value of a woman's unpaid work in the home is often not taken into account in determining divorce settlements and pension benefits. When women turn to the courts to right these wrongs, they are at a distinct disadvantage because of what has and hasn't happened to the Constitution." According to the official NOW statement concerning the ERA, "a constitutional guarantee of equality would absolutely shift the burden away from those fighting discrimination and place it where it belongs, on those who would discriminate. They would have to justify why discrimination should be allowed rather than women having to explain why we deserve equality."

Of course, not all women support the feminist movement. Conservative activist Phyllis Schlafly has been one of its most prominent opponents since the 1960s, and she is widely credited with preventing the ratification of the ERA. Schlafly is also the founder of the Eagle Forum, an organization intended to provide a political alternative for women who do not support feminism. More recently, some social critics have argued that the feminist movement has had a detrimental effect on the American family. They claim that women's growing participation in the workforce has created a void in home life and led to an increase in divorce and single parenthood. Children of working mothers suffer from a lack of parental attention and guidance, these commentators assert, which can have severe effects on their development. Women would do better to concentrate on their children's well-being than to devote themselves single-mindedly to a career, they conclude.

As the second wave of the women's rights movement begins to give way to the third wave—the daughters and granddaughters of the feminists of the 1960s and 1970s—many young feminists would agree with their critics, up to a point. The new generation readily acknowledges that there is no shame in choosing to be a full-time mother and homemaker; what is important to them is that there is a *choice*, that a woman who freely chooses to stay at home during one part of her life is also free to pursue other possibilities later if she should so desire. While the women of the third wave continue to focus on many of the same issues that mobilized the second wave, they are also tackling new problems related to violence, poverty, racism, homophobia, and access to health care. As with prior generations, the women's rights movement is evolving to address the areas of most pressing concern to its members.

As Betty Friedan writes in her autobiography, "The major transformative force, at least for American society in [the twentieth] century,
has been the modern women's movement." The various facets of this
transformative force are explored in *Women's Rights: Contemporary
Issues Companion*. A historical chapter provides an introduction to the
rise of the women's rights movement in the words of its founders.
Additional chapters examine areas of vital importance to the modern
women's rights movement, including discrimination in the workplace
and health care issues. Taking a look outside of the United States, the
anthology also addresses the status of women's rights in the international community. This diverse collection of articles presents a timely
and relevant overview of the problems and challenges faced by
women today.

CHAPTER 1

HISTORIC PERSPECTIVES ON WOMEN'S RIGHTS

Contemporary Issues
Companion

THE DECLARATION OF SENTIMENTS AND RESOLUTIONS

Elizabeth Cady Stanton and the Seneca Falls Convention

In July 1848, a group of women gathered in Seneca Falls, New York, for the first public political meeting that addressed women's rights. At this time, women in the United States could not vote, own property, or attend college, and they were denied access to most professions. Widely regarded as the beginning of the women's movement, the Seneca Falls Convention was organized by Elizabeth Cady Stanton and Lucretia Mott, who were instrumental in the historic fight to secure equality for women. One of the most important results of the convention was the ratification of the Declaration of Sentiments and Resolutions. Modeled after the Declaration of Independence and written primarily by Stanton, the declaration demanded that women be awarded the same rights that were guaranteed to men under the U.S. Constitution. The declaration argued that women should be granted equality with men in all areas of life, including law, education, employment, and the right to vote.

When, in the course of human events, it becomes necessary for one portion of the family of man to assume among the people of the earth a position different from that which they have hitherto occupied, but one to which the laws of nature and of nature's God entitle them, a decent respect to the opinions of mankind requires that they should declare the causes that impel them to such a course.

We hold these truths to be self-evident: that all men and women are created equal; that they are endowed by their Creator with certain inalienable rights; that among these are life, liberty, and the pursuit of happiness; that to secure these rights governments are instituted, deriving their just powers from the consent of the governed. Whenever any form of government becomes destructive of these ends, it is the right of those who suffer from it to refuse allegiance to it, and to insist upon the institution of a new government, laying its foundation on such principles, and organizing its powers in such form, as to

Excerpted from "Declaration of Sentiments and Resolutions," by Elizabeth Cady Stanton and the Seneca Falls Convention, *The History of Woman Suffrage*, vol. I, edited by Elizabeth Cady Stanton, Susan B. Anthony, and Matilda Joslyn Gage (New York: Fowler & Wells, 1881).

them shall seem most likely to effect their safety and happiness.

Prudence, indeed, will dictate that governments long established should not be changed for light and transient causes; and, accordingly, all experience has shown that mankind are more disposed to suffer, while evils are sufferable, than to right themselves by abolishing the forms to which they were accustomed. But when a long train of abuses and usurpations, pursuing invariably the same object, evinces a design to reduce them under absolute despotism, it is their duty to throw off such government and to provide new guards for their future security. Such has been the patient sufferance of the women under this government, and such is now the necessity which constrains them to demand the equal station to which they are entitled.

Woman's Grievances

The history of mankind is a history of repeated injuries and usurpations on the part of man toward woman, having in direct object the establishment of an absolute tyranny over her. To prove this, let facts be submitted to a candid world.

He has never permitted her to exercise her inalienable right to the elective franchise.

He has compelled her to submit to law in the formation of which she had no voice.

He has withheld from her rights which are given to the most ignorant and degraded men, both natives and foreigners.

Having deprived her of this first right as a citizen, the elective franchise, thereby leaving her without representation in the halls of legislation, he has oppressed her on all sides.

He has made her, if married, in the eye of the law, civilly dead.

He has taken from her all right in property, even to the wages she earns.

He has made her morally, an irresponsible being, as she can commit many crimes with impunity, provided they be done in the presence of her husband. In the covenant of marriage, she is compelled to promise obedience to her husband, he becoming, to all intents and purposes, her master—the law giving him power to deprive her of her liberty and to administer chastisement.

He has so framed the laws of divorce, as to what shall be the proper causes and, in case of separation, to whom the guardianship of the children shall be given, as to be wholly regardless of the happiness of the women—the law, in all cases, going upon a false supposition of the supremacy of man and giving all power into his hands.

After depriving her of all rights as a married woman, if single and the owner of property, he has taxed her to support a government which recognizes her only when her property can be made profitable to it.

He has monopolized nearly all the profitable employments, and from those she is permitted to follow, she receives but a scanty remuneration. He closes against her all the avenues to wealth and distinction which he considers most honorable to himself. As a teacher of theology, medicine, or law, she is not known.

He has denied her the facilities for obtaining a thorough education, all colleges being closed against her.

He allows her in church, as well as state, but a subordinate position, claiming apostolic authority for her exclusion from the ministry, and, with some exceptions, from any public participation in the affairs of the church.

He has created a false public sentiment by giving to the world a different code of morals for men and women, by which moral delinquencies which exclude women from society are not only tolerated but deemed of little account in man.

He has usurped the prerogative of Jehovah himself, claiming it as his right to assign for her a sphere of action, when that belongs to her conscience and to her God.

He has endeavored, in every way that he could, to destroy her confidence in her own powers, to lessen her self-respect, and to make her willing to lead a dependent and abject life.

Now, in view of this entire disfranchisement of one-half the people of this country, their social and religious degradation, in view of the unjust laws above mentioned, and because women do feel themselves aggrieved, oppressed, and fraudulently deprived of their most sacred rights, we insist that they have immediate admission to all the rights and privileges which belong to them as citizens of the United States.

In entering upon the great work before us, we anticipate no small amount of misconception, misrepresentation, and ridicule; but we shall use every instrumentality within our power to effect our object. We shall employ agents, circulate tracts, petition the state and national legislatures, and endeavor to enlist the pulpit and the press in our behalf. We hope this Convention will be followed by a series of conventions embracing every part of the country.

Resolutions

Whereas, the great precept of nature is conceded to be that "man shall pursue his own true and substantial happiness." [English jurist William] Blackstone in his *Commentaries* [*on the Laws of England*] remarks that this law of nature, being coeval with mankind and dictated by God himself, is, of course, superior in obligation to any other. It is binding over all the globe, in all countries and at all times; no human laws are of any validity if contrary to this, and such of them as are valid derive all their force, and all their validity, and all their authority, mediately and immediately, from this original; therefore,

Resolved, that such laws as conflict, in any way, with the true and substantial happiness of woman, are contrary to the great precept of nature and of no validity, for this is superior in obligation to any other.

Resolved, that all laws which prevent woman from occupying such a station in society as her conscience shall dictate, or which place her in a position inferior to that of man, are contrary to the great precept of nature and therefore of no force or authority.

Resolved, that woman is man's equal, was intended to be so by the Creator, and the highest good of the race demands that she should be recognized as such.

Resolved, that the women of this country ought to be enlightened in regard to the laws under which they live, that they may no longer publish their degradation by declaring themselves satisfied with their present position, nor their ignorance, by asserting that they have all the rights they want.

Resolved, that inasmuch as man, while claiming for himself intellectual superiority, does accord to woman moral superiority, it is preeminently his duty to encourage her to speak and teach, as she has an opportunity, in all religious assemblies.

Resolved, that the same amount of virtue, delicacy, and refinement of behavior that is required of woman in the social state also be required of man, and the same transgressions should be visited with equal severity on both man and woman.

Resolved, that the objection of indelicacy and impropriety, which is so often brought against woman when she addresses a public audience, comes with a very ill grace from those who encourage, by their attendance, her appearance on the stage, in the concert, or in feats of the circus.

Resolved, that woman has too long rested satisfied in the circumscribed limits which corrupt customs and a perverted application of the Scriptures have marked out for her, and that it is time she should move in the enlarged sphere which her great Creator has assigned her.

Resolved, that it is the duty of the women of this country to secure to themselves their sacred right to the elective franchise.

Resolved, that the equality of human rights results necessarily from the fact of the identity of the race in capabilities and responsibilities.

Resolved, that the speedy success of our cause depends upon the zealous and untiring efforts of both men and women for the overthrow of the monopoly of the pulpit, and for the securing to woman an equal participation with men in the various trades, professions, and commerce.

Resolved, therefore, that, being invested by the Creator with the same capabilities and same consciousness of responsibility for their exercise, it is demonstrably the right and duty of woman, equally with man, to promote every righteous cause by every righteous means; and especially in regard to the great subjects of morals and religion, it is self-evidently her right to participate with her brother in teaching them, both in private and in public, by writing and by speaking, by any instrumentalities proper to be used, and in any assemblies proper to be held; and this being a self-evident truth growing out of the divinely implanted principles of human nature, any custom or authority adverse to it, whether modern or wearing the hoary sanction of antiquity, is to be regarded as a self-evident falsehood, and at war with mankind.

WHY WOMEN SHOULD VOTE

Alice Stone Blackwell

By the early 1900s, the movement to secure women's right to vote had become a strong national force. But at the same time, many people opposed the movement's goals. Common objections to women's suffrage included arguments that women were too uninformed about politics to vote, that most women did not want to vote, and that voting would cause women to neglect their family duties. In the following selection, Alice Stone Blackwell, daughter of the prominent feminist leaders Lucy Stone and Henry Blackwell and an important advocate for suffrage in her own right, counters the opposition by listing sixteen reasons why women should vote. She maintains that suffrage would increase women's knowledge, influence, and experience, while simultaneously improving their lives and the lives of their families.

1. Because it is fair and right that those who must obey the laws should have a voice in making them, and that those who must pay taxes should have a vote as to the size of the tax and the way it shall be spent.

2. Because the moral, educational, and humane legislation desired by women would be got more easily if women had votes. New York women have worked in vain for years to secure a legislative appropriation to found a state industrial School for Girls. Colorado women worked in vain for one till they got the ballot; then the Legislature promptly granted it.

3. Because laws unjust to women would be amended more quickly. It cost Massachusetts women 55 years of effort to secure the law making mothers equal guardians of their children with the fathers. In Colorado, after women were enfranchised, the very next Legislature granted it. After more than half a century of agitation by women for this reform only 13 out of 46 States now give equal guardianship to mothers.

4. Because disfranchisement helps to keep wages down. Hon. Carroll D. Wright, National Commissioner of Labor said in an address delivered at Smith College on February 22, 1902: "The lack of direct

Excerpted from "Why Women Should Vote," by Alice Stone Blackwell, *Political Equality Series*, 1906.

political influence constitutes a powerful reason why women's wages have been kept at a minimum."

5. Because equal suffrage would increase the proportion of educated voters. The high schools of every state in the Union are graduating more girls than boys—often twice or three times as many. (Report of Commissioner of Education.)

6. Because it would increase the proportion of native-born voters. In three years from June 30, 1900, to June 30, 1903, there landed in the United States 1,344,622 foreign men, and only 576,746 foreign women. (Report of Commissioner General of Immigration.)

7. Because it would increase the moral and law-abiding vote very much, while increasing the vicious and criminal vote very little. The U.S. Census of 1890 gives the statistics of men and women in the state prisons of the different States. Omitting fractions, they are as follows: In the District of Columbia, women constitute 17 per cent. of the prisoners; in Massachusetts and Rhode Island, 14 per cent.; in New York, 13; in Louisiana, 12; in Virginia, 11; in New Jersey, 10; in Pennsylvania and Maryland, 9; in Connecticut, 8; in Alabama, New Hampshire, Ohio and South Carolina, 7; in Florida, Maine, Mississippi, New Mexico and Tennessee, 6; in Georgia, Illinois, Indiana, Kentucky, Michigan, Missouri, North Carolina and West Virginia, 5; in Arkansas and Delaware, 4; in California, Minnesota, North Dakota, Texas and Vermont, 3; in Colorado, Iowa, Montana, Nebraska and Utah, 2; in Arizona, Kansas, Nevada and South Dakota, 1; in Washington, four-fifths of 1 per cent.; in Oregon and Wisconsin, two-fifths of 1 per cent.; in Wyoming and Idaho, none.

8. Because it leads to fair treatment of women in the public service. In Massachusetts the average pay of a female teacher is about one-third that of a male teacher, and in almost all the States it is unequal. In Wyoming and Utah, the law provides that they shall receive equal pay for usual work. (Revised Statutes of Wyoming, Section 014; Revised Statutes of Utah, Section 1853.)

9. Because legislation for the protection of children would be secured more easily. Judge [Ben] Lindsey, of the Denver Juvenile Court, writes in [the pro-suffrage journal] *Progress* for July, 1904: "We have in Colorado the most advanced laws of any state in the Union for the care and protection of the home and the children. These laws in my opinion, would not exist at this time if it were not for the powerful influence of woman suffrage."

10. Because it is the quietest, easiest, most dignified and least conspicuous way of influencing public affairs. It takes much less expenditure of time, labor and personal presence to go up to the ballot box, drop in a slip of paper, and then come away, than to persuade a multitude of miscellaneous voters to vote right.

11. Because it would make women more broadminded. Professor Edward H. Griggs says: "The ballot is an educator, and women will

become more practical and more wise in using it."

12. Because woman's ballot will make it hard for the notoriously bad candidates to be nominated or elected. In the equal suffrage states, both parties have to put men of respectable character or lose the women's vote.

13. Because it would increase women's influence. Mrs. Mary C.C. Bradford, president of the Colorado State Federation of Women's Clubs, said at the National Suffrage Convention in Washington in February [1904]: "Instead of woman's influence being lessened by the ballot, it is greatly increased. Last year there were so many members of the legislature with bills which they wanted the club women to indorse that the Social Science department of the State Federation had to sit one day each week to confer with these legislators who were seeking our endorsement. Club women outside the suffrage states do not have this experience."

14. Because it would help those women who need help the most. Theodore Roosevelt recommended woman suffrage in his message to the New York Legislature. On being asked why, he reported to have answered that many women have a very hard time, working women especially, and if the ballot would help them, even a little, he was willing to see it tried. Mrs. Maud Nathan, President of the National Consumers League, said in an address at the National Suffrage Convention in Washington, in February, 1904: "My experience in investigating the condition of women wage-earners warrants the assertion that some of the evils from which they suffer would not exist if women had the ballot. . . . In the States women vote, there is far better enforcement of the laws which protect working girls."

15. Because it is a maxim in war. "Always do the thing to which your adversary particularly objects." Every vicious interest in the country would rather continue to contend with woman's indirect influence than try to cope with woman's vote.

16. Because experience has proved it to be good. Women have for years been voting literally by hundreds of thousands, in England, Scotland, Ireland, Australia, New Zealand, Canada, Wyoming, Colorado, Kansas, Utah, and Idaho, in all these places put together, the opponents have not yet found a dozen respectable men who assert over their own names and addresses that the results have been bad, while scores of prominent men and women testify that it has done good. An ounce of fret is worth a ton of theory.

WOMEN HAVE NO NEED TO VOTE

Grace Duffield Goodwin

Not all American women wanted the right to vote, and many actively opposed the suffrage movement. Grace Duffield Goodwin was one of these opponents. In the following excerpt from her book *Anti-Suffrage: Ten Good Reasons*, Goodwin takes issue with the characterization of voting as a right. Rather, she insists, voting is a responsibility—one that men shoulder so that women can devote their time and energy to family and household duties. She maintains that political issues are too complicated and time-consuming for women to deal with. A few states have already granted women the right to vote, Goodwin explains, and the results have been disastrous. She concludes that granting women suffrage would be dangerous for them, their families, and the government.

In early days, long before the [Civil] war, the great question of slavery aroused the interest of some few far-sighted American men and women, and at an international abolition conference held in London, such men as William Lloyd Garrison and Wendell Phillips went as delegates. With them were appointed several brilliant women, friends and counsellors of those men: Lucretia Mott, Elizabeth Cady Stanton, and others. On reaching London, the women were refused official recognition, which so incensed Garrison that he arose and left the hall. On the return of the party to this country, there was set on foot the Woman's Rights movement, which for awhile swept the land like wild-fire. The women rightly felt that they should have been allowed to vote upon this important issue. The agitation, therefore, had its origin among noble and brilliant people for great moral ends, and, in the passage of time, has gathered to itself gradually a younger group of adherents, who have forced it far beyond its original purpose, who have failed to remark the growing complication of political problems, and who cannot be made to realize that today the great issues on which the original demand was based, have so changed that what was once a question of the best way to handle a moral issue has now become a question of the best way to handle party politics. At the pre-

Excerpted from *Anti-Suffrage: Ten Good Reasons*, by Grace Duffield Goodwin (New York: Duffield and Company, 1913).

sent time this question of woman suffrage is not a question of one clear-cut moral issue, not a question of the theory of government or the philosophy of government, but simply and solely a question of politics. Given the highly specialized profession of politics, the "great game," played as it is now in this country, will the entrance of women into the field make it better or worse? By doubling the electorate, and therefore, according to the law of averages, coming out with conditions very little changed, can we hope to do anything more than make more difficult an already difficult task?

"Educating by means of the ballot" is an experiment to be tried slowly, and not by throwing into our electorate a mass of indifferent and inexperienced voters. Those who steadily oppose this experiment consider it far too difficult and dangerous to be thrust upon a nation which has so recently won its title to be considered a world-power. America is a vigorous young leader in the family of nations. It should not have its progress checked by rash ventures which have to do with the very foundations of its governmental life.

Voting Is a Responsibility, Not a Right

In considering this question fairly, we must understand that there is no such thing as a "natural right" to the ballot. Natural rights are rights to life, property, etc.; the ballot is a man-devised instrument for the peaceful expression of the popular will in government. It is conferred as a serious responsibility upon men who have fulfilled certain well-known conditions. Women are made *exempt* from the exercise of political responsibility in view of the duties toward home and family which they are performing for the benefit of the state. *The ballot is not a right denied; it is a burden removed.* . . . Great confusion has existed on this point, but there is really no reason at all for anything but an acknowledgment of the facts.

The ballot being a responsibility, if we demand it and receive it we must be prepared to accept all that it entails, and the state must be prepared also to accept the difficulties and dangers which will arise from a sudden and great enlargement of the voting body.

We have been told, even by such men as the late Senator [George F.] Hoar [who was an advocate for women's suffrage], that if women receive the franchise they may vote or not, as they desire. This is not the original conception of the duty of a voter. Men are never so taught. Everywhere they are urged to vote, and the pulpits of the land make the casting of a ballot a patriotic and religious duty. The late Ex-Governor [George H.] Utter of Rhode Island claims that one of the greatest dangers will be the enlargement of the indifferent class, the busy, middle-class tradesman and housekeeper. Men of this type, he says, are already a great drag on elections, and have always to be brought to the polls by those interested in "getting out the vote."

The ballot carries with it the duty of bearing arms in time of war, and of jury duty in times of peace. If women are granted the ballot the governmental system will have to be reconstructed to free us from these duties, or we shall have to attend to them while doing our own peculiar and non-transferable tasks. Mr. William Allen's frivolous argument, in his "Woman's Part in Government," to the effect that any woman can bear arms who can struggle with the crush at the Brooklyn bridge, is wide of the mark. Absence from home and children during prolonged jury service will not materially help the state. Women are everywhere today suffering from exhaustion of vital force, due to the incessant demands of a life crowded with claims outside the home, either in social obligations, philanthropic or civic interests, or the taxing strain of industrial life. Between these two comes the large percentage of American women, far larger than any other class, who need all their strength for necessary household tasks. The watchful and intelligent observer fails to see the surplus of strength to be expended in a man's way for the good of the state, and he does see the good of the state seriously menaced at its source by the inroads upon feminine vitality which will be made when political duties are added to those bound upon our shoulders first by nature, second by a highly developed civilization. This applies not so much to those women who would be content merely to vote, as to that large class which would inevitably, in its natural desire for power and publicity, "enter politics."

The suffragists remind us that the political burden is not heavy for the average man; that he spends very little time and energy in governing his country. In every community, however, from village to city, there are men who "handle the politics," and who give up their lives to it, degrading themselves as bosses and grafters, or wearing themselves out as reformers. The same number of women would in all probability do the same things, because every manhood class has either a corresponding or a potentially corresponding womanhood class, and this proportion of women is too large to be needlessly sacrificed.

Political Corruption and Women

The "woman in politics" is not a menace of the future. She has appeared, and if she be a type, it is instructive to look upon her and see to what more politics will lead. Women in politics are like men in politics—so testify Judge [Ben] Lindsey and Gen. Irving Hale, both of Colorado [where women had the right to vote]. They are good, bad and indifferent, with the added emphasis of the tendency to the extreme inherent in all women, so that a woman corrupt in politics has been shown to be worse than a man; a woman to gain political ends has been known to offer what is euphemistically, but quite clearly described as the "new bribery"—an abyss of horror into which only the lowest will fall, but into which the lowest *will* fall, as they fell in the days of the Roman decadence. We cannot afford to have any woman so besmirched.

In considering this question it is well to observe all its aspects. The opponents of suffrage for women are deeply convinced that there are elements of danger for some women that all women should consider, and elements of danger for the state that should be matter of consideration for both men and women, before we commit this country, unique in history and in composition, to an experiment in which is undeniable danger both to government and to women.

WOMEN'S RIGHT TO BIRTH CONTROL

Margaret Sanger

Margaret Sanger, founder of Planned Parenthood, passionately
believed that women had the right to choose whether or not to
have children. The Comstock Law of 1873 prohibited women
from even obtaining information about contraception, much less
actual birth control devices. In defiance of the law, Sanger began
to illegally distribute information and contraceptive devices so
that women would not have to suffer the negative consequences
of unwanted multiple pregnancies. In the following excerpt from
her 1920 book *Woman and the New Race*, Sanger argues that
women have not only a right to knowledge about contraception,
but also a responsibility to practice wise family planning. Women
cannot be truly free, she insists, until they have complete control
over their bodies.

The problem of birth control has arisen directly from the effort of the
feminine spirit to free itself from bondage. Woman herself has
wrought that bondage through her reproductive powers and while
enslaving herself has enslaved the world. The physical suffering to be
relieved is chiefly woman's. Hers, too, is the love life that dies first
under the blight of too prolific breeding. Within her is wrapped up
the future of the race—it is hers to make or mar. All of these considerations point unmistakably to one fact—it is woman's duty as well as
her privilege to lay hold of the means of freedom. Whatever men may
do, she cannot escape the responsibility. For ages she has been
deprived of the opportunity to meet this obligation. She is now
emerging from her helplessness. Even as no one can share the suffering of the overburdened mother, so no one can do this work for her.
Others may help, but she and she alone can free herself.

Birth Control and Freedom

The basic freedom of the world is woman's freedom. A free race cannot be born of slave mothers. A woman enchained cannot choose but
give a measure of that bondage to her sons and daughters. No woman
can call herself free who does not own and control her body. No

Excerpted from *Woman and the New Race*, by Margaret Sanger (New York: Brentano's,
1920).

woman can call herself free until she can choose consciously whether she will or will not be a mother.

It does not greatly alter the case that some women call themselves free because they earn their own livings, while others profess freedom because they defy the conventions of sex relationship. She who earns her own living gains a sort of freedom that is not to be undervalued, but in quality and in quantity it is of little account beside the untrammeled choice of mating or not mating, of being a mother or not being a mother. She gains food and clothing and shelter, at least, without submitting to the charity of her companion, but the earning of her own living does not give her the development of her inner sex urge, far deeper and more powerful in its outworkings than any of these externals. In order to have that development, she must still meet and solve the problem of motherhood.

With the so-called "free" woman, who chooses a mate in defiance of convention, freedom is largely a question of character and audacity. If she does attain to an unrestricted choice of a mate, she is still in a position to be enslaved through her reproductive powers. Indeed, the pressure of law and custom upon the woman not legally married is likely to make her more of a slave than the woman fortunate enough to marry the man of her choice.

Look at it from any standpoint you will, suggest any solution you will, conventional or unconventional, sanctioned by law or in defiance of law, woman is in the same position, fundamentally, until she is able to determine for herself whether she will be a mother and to fix the number of her offspring. This unavoidable situation is alone enough to make birth control, first of all, a woman's problem. On the very face of the matter, voluntary motherhood is chiefly the concern of the woman.

It is persistently urged, however, that since sex expression is the act of two, the responsibility of controlling the results should not be placed upon woman alone. Is it fair, it is asked, to give her, instead of the man, the task of protecting herself when she is, perhaps, less rugged in physique than her mate, and has, at all events, the normal, periodic inconveniences of her sex?

The Ideal Versus the Reality

We must examine this phase of her problem in two lights—that of the ideal, and of the conditions working toward the ideal. In an ideal society, no doubt, birth control would become the concern of the man as well as the woman. The hard, inescapable fact which we encounter to-day is that man has not only refused any such responsibility, but has individually and collectively sought to prevent woman from obtaining knowledge by which she could assume this responsibility for herself. She is still in the position of a dependent to-day because her mate has refused to consider her as an individual apart from his needs. She is still bound because she has in the past left the solution of the problem to him. Having left it to him, she finds that instead of rights, she has only such privileges as she has gained by petitioning, coaxing and cozening. Having left it to him, she is exploited, driven and enslaved to his desires.

While it is true that he suffers many evils as the consequence of this situation, she suffers vastly more. While it is true that he should be awakened to the cause of these evils, we know that they come home to her with crushing force every day. It is she who has the long burden of carrying, bearing and rearing the unwanted children. It is she who must watch beside the beds of pain where lie the babies who suffer because they have come into overcrowded homes. It is her heart that the sight of the deformed, the subnormal, the undernourished, the overworked child smites first and oftenest and hardest. It is *her* love life that dies first in the fear of undesired pregnancy. It is her opportunity for self expression that perishes first and most hopelessly because of it.

Conditions, rather than theories, facts, rather than dreams, govern the problem. They place it squarely upon the shoulders of woman. She has learned that whatever the moral responsibility of the man in this direction may be, he does not discharge it. She has learned that, lovable and considerate as the individual husband may be, she has nothing to expect from men in the mass, when they make laws and decree customs. She knows that regardless of what ought to be, the brutal unavoidable fact is that she will never receive her freedom until she takes it for herself.

Women Must Remake the World

Having learned this much, she has yet something more to learn. Women are too much inclined to follow in the footsteps of men, to try to think as men think, to try to solve the general problems of life as men solve them. If after attaining their freedom, women accept conditions in the spheres of government, industry, art, morals and religion as they find them, they will be but taking a leaf out of man's book. The woman is not needed to do man's work. She is not needed to think man's thoughts. She need not fear that the masculine mind, almost universally dominant, will fail to take care of its own. Her mission is not to enhance the masculine spirit, but to express the feminine; hers is not to preserve a man-made world, but to create a human world by the infusion of the feminine element into all of its activities.

Woman must not accept; she must challenge. She must not be awed by that which has been built up around her; she must reverence that within her which struggles for expression. Her eyes must be less upon what is and more clearly upon what should be. She must listen only with a frankly questioning attitude to the dogmatized opinions of man-made society. When she chooses her new, free course of action, it must be in the light of her own opinion—of her own intuition. Only so can she give play to the feminine spirit. Only thus can she free her mate from the bondage which he wrought for himself when he wrought hers. Only thus can she restore to him that of which he robbed himself in restricting her. Only thus can she remake the world.

The world is, indeed, hers to remake, it is hers to build and to recreate. Even as she has permitted the suppression of her own feminine element and the consequent impoverishment of industry, art, letters, science, morals, religions and social intercourse, so it is hers to enrich all these.

Woman must have her freedom—the fundamental freedom of choosing whether or not she shall be a mother and how many children she will have. Regardless of what man's attitude may be, that problem is hers—and before it can be his, it is hers alone.

She goes through the vale of death alone, each time a babe is born. As it is the right neither of man nor the state to coerce her into this ordeal, so it is her right to decide whether she will endure it. That right to decide imposes upon her the duty of clearing the way to knowledge by which she may make and carry out the decision.

Birth control is woman's problem. The quicker she accepts it as hers and hers alone, the quicker will society respect motherhood. The quicker, too, will the world be made a fit place for her children to live.

WHAT IT WOULD BE LIKE IF WOMEN WIN

Gloria Steinem

After the Nineteenth Amendment legalizing women's suffrage was signed into law in 1920, the women's rights movement moved into a period of dormancy. However, by the 1960s, women were again beginning to question their status in American society. The women's rights movement entered a "second wave" in which women began fighting for equality in the workplace, politics, and the law. In addition, many feminists challenged what they saw as widespread sexist attitudes. In this 1970 essay, feminist activist and author Gloria Steinem offers a vision of what the world would be like if women achieved true equality with men. She maintains that equality would make the world a better place for both women and men, with each bearing an equal share of responsibility for the family, in the workplace, and throughout society.

Any change is fearful, especially one affecting both politics and sex roles, so let me begin these utopian speculations with a fact. To break the ice.

Women don't want to exchange places with men. Male chauvinists, science-fiction writers and comedians may favor that idea for its shock value, but psychologists say it is a fantasy based on the ruling-class ego and guilt. Men assume that women want to imitate them, which is just what white people assumed about blacks. An assumption so strong that it may convince the second-class group of the need to imitate, but for both women and blacks that stage has passed. Guilt produces the question. What if they could treat us as we have treated them?

That is not our goal. But we do want to change the economic system to one more based on merit. In Women's Lib Utopia, there will be free access to good jobs—and decent pay for the bad ones women have been performing all along, including housework. Increased skilled labor might lead to a four-hour workday, and higher wages would encourage further mechanization of repetitive jobs now kept alive by cheap labor.

With women as half the country's elected representatives, and a woman President once in a while, the country's *machismo* problems would be greatly reduced. The old-fashioned idea that manhood depends on violence and victory is, after all, an important part of our troubles in the streets, and in Viet Nam. I'm not saying that women leaders would eliminate violence. We are not more moral than men; we are only uncorrupted by power so far. When we do acquire power, we might turn out to have an equal impulse toward aggression. Even now, [anthropologist] Margaret Mead believes that women fight less often but more fiercely than men, because women are not taught the rules of the war game and fight only when cornered. But for the next 50 years or so, women in politics will be very valuable by tempering the idea of manhood into something less aggressive and better suited to this crowded, post-atomic planet. Consumer protection and children's rights, for instance, might get more legislative attention.

Men will have to give up ruling-class privileges, but in return they will no longer be the only ones to support the family, get drafted, bear the strain of power and responsibility. Freud to the contrary, anatomy is not destiny, at least not for more than nine months at a time. In Israel, women are drafted, and some have gone to war. In England, more men type and run switchboards. In India and Israel, a woman rules. In Sweden, both parents take care of the children. In this country, come Utopia, men and women won't reverse roles; they will be free to choose according to individual talents and preferences.

If role reform sounds sexually unsettling, think how it will change the sexual hypocrisy we have now. No more sex arranged on the barter system, with women pretending interest, and men never sure whether they are loved for themselves or for the security few women can get any other way. (Married or not, for sexual reasons or social ones, most women still find it second nature to Uncle-Tom.) No more men who are encouraged to spend a lifetime living with inferiors; with housekeepers, or dependent creatures who are still children. No more domineering wives, emasculating women, and "Jewish mothers," all of whom are simply human beings with all their normal ambition and drive confined to the home. No more unequal partnerships that eventually doom love and sex.

In order to produce that kind of confidence and individuality, child rearing will train according to talent. Little girls will no longer be surrounded by air-tight, self-fulfilling prophecies of natural passivity, lack of ambition and objectivity, inability to exercise power, and dexterity (so long as special aptitude for jobs requiring patience and dexterity is confined to poorly paid jobs; brain surgery is for males).

Schools and universities will help to break down traditional sex roles, even when parents will not. Half the teachers will be men, a rarity now at preschool and elementary levels; girls will not necessarily serve cookies or boys hoist up the flag. Athletic teams will be picked

only by strength and skill. Sexually segregated courses like auto
mechanics and home economics will be taken by boys and girls
together. New courses in sexual politics will explore female subjuga-
tion as the model for political oppression, and women's history will
be an academic staple, along with black history, at least until the
white-male-oriented textbooks are integrated and rewritten.

As for the American child's classic problem—too much mother, too
little father—that would be cured by an equalization of parental
responsibility. Free nurseries, school lunches, family cafeterias built
into every housing complex, service companies that will do household cleaning chores in a regular, businesslike way, and more responsibility by the entire community for the children: all these will make
it possible for both mother and father to work, and to have equal
leisure time with the children at home. For parents of very young
children, however, a special job category, created by Government and
unions, would allow such parents a shorter work day.

The revolution would not take away the option of being a housewife. A woman who prefers to be her husband's housekeeper and/or
hostess would receive a percentage of his pay determined by the domestic relations courts. If divorced, she might be eligible for a pension fund,
and for a job-training allowance. Or a divorce could be treated the same
way that the dissolution of a business partnership is now.

If these proposals seem farfetched, consider Sweden, where most of
them are already in effect. Sweden is not yet a working Women's Lib
model; most of the role-reform programs began less than a decade
ago, and are just beginning to take hold. But that country is so far
ahead of us in recognizing the problem that Swedish statements on
sex and equality sound like bulletins from the moon.

Our marriage laws, for instance, are so reactionary that Women's
Lib groups want couples to take a compulsory written exam on the
law, as for a driver's license, before going through with the wedding. A
man has alimony and wifely debts to worry about, but a woman may
lose so many of her civil rights that in the U.S. now, in important
legal ways, she becomes a child again. In some states, she cannot sign
credit agreements, use her maiden name, incorporate a business, or
establish a legal residence of her own. Being a wife, according to most
social and legal definitions, is still a 19th century thing.

Assuming, however, that these blatantly sexist laws are abolished or
reformed, that job discrimination is forbidden, that parents share financial responsibility for each other and the children, and that sexual relationships become partnerships of equal adults (some pretty big assumptions), then marriage will probably go right on. Men and women are,
after all, physically complementary. When society stops encouraging
men to be exploiters and women to be parasites, they may turn out to
be more complementary in emotion as well. Women's Lib is not trying
to destroy the American family. A look at the statistics on divorce—plus

the way in which old people are farmed out with strangers and young people flee the home—shows the destruction that has already been done. Liberated women are just trying to point out the disaster, and build compassionate and practical alternatives from the ruins.

What will exist is a variety of alternative life-styles. Since the population explosion dictates that childbearing be kept to a minimum, parents-and-children will be only one of many "families": couples, age groups, working groups, mixed communes, blood-related clans, class groups, creative groups. Single women will have the right to stay single without ridicule, without the attitudes now betrayed by "spinster" and "bachelor." Lesbians or homosexuals will no longer be denied legally binding marriages, complete with mutual-support agreements and inheritance rights. Paradoxically, the number of homosexuals may get smaller. With fewer overpossessive mothers and fewer fathers who hold up an impossibly cruel or perfectionist idea of manhood, boys will be less likely to be denied or reject their identity as males.

Changes that now seem small may get bigger:

Men's Lib

Men now suffer from more diseases due to stress, heart attacks, ulcers, a higher suicide rate, greater difficulty living alone, less adaptability to change and, in general, a shorter life span than women. There is some scientific evidence that what produces physical problems is not work itself, but the inability to choose which work, and how much. With women bearing half the financial responsibility, and with the idea of "masculine" jobs gone, men might well feel freer and live longer.

Religion

Protestant women are already becoming ordained ministers; radical nuns are carrying out liturgical functions that were once the exclusive property of priests; Jewish women are rewriting prayers—particularly those that Orthodox Jews recite every morning thanking God they are not female. In the future, the church will become an area of equal participation by women. This means, of course, that organized religion will have to give up one of its great historical weapons: sexual repression. In most structured faiths, from Hinduism through Roman Catholicism, the status of women went down as the position of priests ascended. Male clergy implied, if they did not teach, that women were unclean, unworthy and sources of ungodly temptation, in order to remove them as rivals for the emotional forces of men. Full participation of women in ecclesiastical life might involve certain changes in theology, such as, for instance, a radical redefinition of sin.

Literary Problems

Revised sex roles will outdate more children's books than civil rights ever did. Only a few children had the problem of a *Little Black Sambo*, but most have the male-female stereotypes of "Dick and Jane." A boomlet of children's books about mothers who work has already begun, and liberated parents and editors are beginning to pressure for change in the textbook industry. Fiction writing will change more gradually, but romantic novels with wilting heroines and swashbuckling heroes will be reduced to historical value. Or perhaps to the sadomasochist trade. (*Marjorie Morningstar*, a romantic novel that took the '50s by storm, has already begun to seem as unreal as its '20s predecessor, *The Sheik*.) As for the literary plots that turn on forced marriages or horrific abortions, they will seem as dated as Prohibition stories. Free legal abortions and free birth control will force writers to give up pregnancy as the *deus ex machina*.

Manners and Fashion

Dress will be more androgynous, with class symbols becoming more important than sexual ones. Pro- or anti-Establishment styles may already be more vital than who is wearing them. Hardhats are just as likely to rough up antiwar girls as antiwar men in the street, and police understand that women are just as likely to be pushers or bombers. Dances haven't required that one partner lead the other for years, anyway. Chivalry will transfer itself to those who need it, or deserve respect: old people, admired people, anyone with an armload of packages. Women with normal work identities will be less likely to attach their whole sense of self to youth and appearance; thus there will be fewer nervous breakdowns when the first wrinkles appear. Lighting cigarettes and other treasured niceties will become gestures of mutual affection. "I like to be helped on with my coat," says one Women's Lib worker, "but not if it costs me $2,000 a year in salary."

For those with nostalgia for a simpler past, here is a word of comfort. Anthropologist Geoffrey Gofer studied the few peaceful human tribes and discovered one common characteristic: sex roles were not polarized. Differences of dress and occupation were at a minimum. Society, in other words, was not using sexual blackmail as a way of getting women to do cheap labor, or men to be aggressive.

Thus Women's Lib may achieve a more peaceful society on the way toward its other goals. That is why the Swedish government considers reform to bring about greater equality in the sex roles one of its most important concerns. As Prime Minister Olof Palme explained in a widely ignored speech delivered in Washington this spring: "It is *human beings* we shall emancipate. In Sweden today, if a politician should declare that the woman ought to have a different role from man's, he would be regarded as something from the Stone Age." In other words, the most radical goal of the movement is egalitarianism.

If Women's Lib wins, perhaps we all do.

HONORING THE PAST, IMAGINING THE FUTURE

Hillary Rodham Clinton

In July 1998, then–First Lady Hillary Rodham Clinton delivered the following speech at the commemoration of the 150th anniversary of the first women's rights convention in Seneca Falls, New York. The fight for women's equality begun at Seneca Falls is still a relevant one today, Clinton maintains. While Clinton acknowledges that many improvements have taken place since then, she contends that much work remains to be done to secure women's access to equal education, employment, health care, and financial security. In order to achieve these goals, Clinton encourages women to exercise their right to vote and to continue to work for a future of equality for all people. Clinton is currently a U.S. senator representing New York.

For a moment, I would like you to take your minds back 150 years. Imagine if you will that you are Charlotte Woodward, a 19-year-old glove-maker working and living in Waterloo [New York]. Every day you sit for hours sewing gloves together, working for small wages you cannot even keep, with no hope of going on in school or owning property, knowing that if you marry, your children and even the clothes on your body will belong to your husband.

But then one day in July 1848, you hear about a women's rights convention to be held in nearby Seneca Falls. It's a convention to discuss the "social, civil, and religious conditions and rights of women." You run from house to house and you find other women who have heard the same news. Some are excited, others are amused or even shocked, and a few agree to come with you, for at least the first day.

When that day comes—July 19, 1848—you leave early in the morning in your horse-drawn wagon. You fear that no one else will come, and at first, the road is empty, except for you and your neighbors. But suddenly, as you reach a crossroads, you see a few more wagons and carriages, then more and more, all going toward Wesleyan Chapel. Eventually you join the others to form one long procession on the road to equality.

Excerpted from Hillary Rodham Clinton's remarks at the 150th Anniversary of the First Women's Rights Convention, July 16, 1998.

The Road to Seneca Falls

Who were the others traveling that road to equality, traveling to that
convention? Frederick Douglass, the former slave and great abolition-
ist, was on his way there and he described the participants as "few in
numbers, moderate in resources, and very little-known in the world.
The most we had to connect us was a firm commitment that we were
in the right and a firm faith that the right must ultimately prevail." In
the wagons and carriages, on foot or horseback, were women like
Rhoda Palmer. Seventy years later in 1918, at the age of 102, she
would cast her first ballot in a New York state election.

Also traveling down that road to equality was Susan Quinn, who at
15 will become the youngest signer of the Declaration of Sentiments.
Catherine Fish-Steben, a veteran of activism starting when she was
only 12 going door to door collecting anti-slavery petitions. She also,
by the way, kept an anti-tobacco pledge on the parlor table and asked
all her young male friends to sign up. She was a woman truly ahead of
her time, as all the participants were.

I often wonder, when reflecting back on the Seneca Falls Convention, who of us—men and women—would have left our homes, our
families, our work, to make that journey 150 years ago. Think about
the incredible courage it must have taken to join that procession.
Ordinary men and women, mothers and fathers, sisters and brothers,
husbands and wives, friends and neighbors. And just like those who
have embarked on other journeys throughout American history, seeking freedom or escaping religious or political persecution, speaking
out against slavery, working for labor rights, these men and women
were motivated by dreams of better lives and more just societies.

At the end of the two-day convention, 100 people, 68 women and
32 men, signed the Declaration of Sentiments that you can now read
on the wall at Wesleyan Chapel. Among the signers were some of the
names we remember today: Elizabeth Cady Stanton and Lucretia
Mott, Martha Wright and Frederick Douglass and young Charlotte
Woodward. The "Seneca Falls 100," as I like to call them, shared the
radical idea that America fell far short of her ideals stated in our
founding documents, denying citizenship to women and slaves.

Elizabeth Cady Stanton, who is frequently credited with originating
the idea for the convention, knew that women were not only denied
legal citizenship, but that society's cultural values and social structures
conspired to assign women only one occupation and role, that of wife
and mother. Of course, the reality was always far different. Women
have always worked, and worked both in the home and outside the
home for as long as history can record. And even though Stanton herself had a comfortable life and valued deeply her husband and seven
children, she knew that she and all other women were not truly free if
they could not keep wages they earned, divorce an abusive husband,
own property, or vote for the political leaders who governed them.

Stanton was inspired along with the others who met to rewrite our Declaration of Independence, and they boldly asserted, "We hold these truths to be self-evident that all men and women are created equal."

Women's Rights, Past and Present

"All men and all women." It was the shout heard around the world, and if we listen, we can still hear its echoes today. We can hear it in the voices of women demanding their full civil and political rights anywhere in the world. I've heard such voices and their echoes from women around the world, from Belfast to Bosnia to Beijing, as they work to change the conditions for women and girls and improve their lives and the lives of their families. We can even hear those echoes today in Seneca Falls. We come together this time not by carriage, but by car or plane, by train or foot, and yes, in my case, by bus. We come together not to hold a convention, but to celebrate those who met here 150 years ago, to commemorate how far we have traveled since then, and to challenge ourselves to persevere on the journey that was begun all those many years ago. . . .

Because we must tell and retell, learn and relearn these women's stories, we must make it our personal mission, in our everyday lives, to pass these stories on to our daughters and sons. Because we cannot—we must not—ever forget that the rights and opportunities that we enjoy as women today were not just bestowed upon us by some benevolent ruler. They were fought for, agonized over, marched for, jailed for, and even died for by brave and persistent women and men who came before us.

Every time we buy or sell or inherit property in our own name—let us thank the pioneers who agitated to change the laws that made that possible.

Every time we vote, let us thank the women and men of Seneca Falls, Susan B. Anthony, and all the others who tirelessly crossed our nation and withstood ridicule and the rest to bring about the 19th Amendment to the Constitution.

Every time we enter an occupation—a profession of our own choosing—and receive a paycheck that reflects earnings equal to a male colleague, let us thank the signers. . . .

Every time we elect a woman to office—let us thank groundbreaking leaders like Jeanette Rankin and Margaret Chase Smith, Patti Caraway, Louise Slaughter, Bella Abzug, Shirley Chrisholm—all of whom proved that a woman's place is truly in the House, and in the Senate, and one day, in the White House, as well.

And every time we take another step forward for justice in this nation—let us thank extraordinary women like Harriet Tubman, . . . who escaped herself from slavery, and then risked her life, time and again, to bring at least 200 other slaves to freedom as well.

Harriet Tubman's rule for all of her underground railroad missions was to keep going. Once you started—no matter how scared you got, how dangerous it became—you were not allowed to turn back. That's a pretty good rule for life. It not only describes the women who gathered in Wesleyan Chapel in 1848, but it could serve as our own motto for today. We, too, cannot turn back. We, too, must keep going in our commitment to the dignity of every individual—to women's rights as human rights. We are on that road of the pioneers to Seneca Falls: they started down it 150 years ago. But now, we too, must keep going.

We may not face the criticism and derision they did. They understood that the Declaration of Sentiments would create no small amount of misconception, or misrepresentation and ridicule; they were called mannish women, old maids, fanatics, attacked personally by those who disagreed with them. One paper said, "These rights for women would bring a monstrous injury to all mankind." If it sounds familiar, it's the same thing that's always said when women keep going for true equality and justice.

Those who came here also understood that the convention and the Declaration were only first steps down that road. What matters most is what happens when everyone packs up and goes back to their families and communities. What matters is whether sentiment and resolutions, once made, are fulfilled or forgotten. The Seneca Falls 100 pledged themselves to petition, and lit the pulpit and used every instrumentality within their power to affect their subjects. And they did. But they also knew they were not acting primarily for themselves. They knew they probably would not even see the changes they advocated in their own lifetime. In fact, only Charlotte Woodward lived long enough to see American women finally win the right to vote.

Those who signed that Declaration were doing it for the girls and women—for us—those of us in the 20th century.

Elizabeth Cady Stanton wrote a letter to her daughters later in life enclosing a special gift and explaining why. "Dear Maggie and Patti, this is my first speech," she wrote, "it contains all I knew at that time. I give this manuscript to my precious daughters in the hopes that they will finish the work that I have begun." And they have. Her daughter, Harriet Blatch, was the chief strategist of the suffrage movement in New York. Harriet's daughter, Nova Barney, was one of the first women to be a civil engineer. Nora's daughter, Rhoda Jenkins, became an architect. Rhoda's daughter, Colleen Jenkins-Salen is an elected official in Greenwich, Connecticut. And her daughter, Elizabeth, is a 13-year-old who wrote about the six generations of Stantons in a book called, *33 Things Every Child Should Know.*

The Future of Women's Rights

So, far into the 20th century, the work is still being done; the journey goes on. Now, some might say that the only purpose of this celebration is to honor the past, that the work begun here is finished in

America, that young women no longer face legal obstacles to whatever education or employment choices they choose to pursue. And I certainly believe and hope all of you agree that we should, every day, count our blessings as American women.

I know how much change I have seen in my own life. When I was growing up back in the 1950s and 1960s, there were still barriers that Mrs. Stanton would have recognized—scholarships I couldn't apply for, schools I couldn't go to, jobs I couldn't have—just because of my sex. Thanks to federal laws like the Civil Rights Act of 1964 and Title IX and the Equal Pay Act, legal barriers to equality have fallen.

But if all we do is honor the past, then I believe we will miss the central point of the Declaration of Sentiments, which was, above all, a document about the future. The drafters of the Declaration imagined a different future for women and men, in a society based on equality and mutual respect. It falls to every generation to imagine the future, and it is our task to do so now.

We know that, just as the women 150 years ago knew, that what we imagine will be principally for our daughters and sons in the 21st century. Because the work of the Seneca Falls Convention is, just like the work of the nation itself, never finished, so long as there remain gaps between our ideals and reality. That is one of the great joys and beauties of the American experiment. We are always striving to build and move toward a more perfect union, that we on every occasion keep faith with our founding ideals, and translate them into reality. So what kind of future can we imagine together?

Finishing the Work of Seneca Falls

If we are to finish the work begun here—then no American should ever again face discrimination on the basis of gender, race, or sexual orientation anywhere in our country.

If we are to finish the work begun here—then 76 cents in a woman's paycheck for every dollar in a man's is still not enough. Equal pay for equal work can once and for all be achieved.

If we are to finish the work begun here—then families need more help to balance their responsibilities at work and at home. In a letter to Susan B. Anthony, Elizabeth Cady Stanton writes, "Come here and I will do what I can to help you with your address, if you will hold the baby and make the pudding." Even then, women knew we had to have help with child care. All families should have access to safe, affordable, quality child care.

If we are to finish the work begun here—then women and children must be protected against what the Declaration called the "chastisement of women," namely domestic abuse and violence. We must take all steps necessary to end the scourge of violence against women and punish the perpetrators. And our country must join the rest of the world, as so eloquently Secretary [of State Madeline] Albright called for on Saturday night here in Seneca Falls, "Join the rest of the world and ratify the [United Nations] convention on the elimination of discrimination against women."

If we are to finish the work begun here—we must do more than talk about family values. We must adopt policies that truly value families—policies like a universal system of healthcare insurance that guarantees every American's access to affordable, quality healthcare. Policies like taking all steps necessary to keep guns out of the hands of children and criminals. Policies like doing all that is necessary at all levels of our society to ensure high-quality public education for every boy or girl, no matter where that child lives.

If we are to finish the work begun here—we must ensure that women and men who work full-time earn a wage that lifts them out of poverty and all workers who retire have financial security in their later years through guaranteed Social Security and pensions.

If we are to finish the work begun here—we must be vigilant against the messages of a media-driven consumer culture that convinces our sons and daughters that what brand of sneakers they wear or cosmetics they use is more important that what they think, feel, know, or do.

And if we are to finish the work begun here—we must, above all else, take seriously the power of the vote and use it to make our voices heard. What the champions of suffrage understood was that the vote is not just a symbol of our equality, but that it can be, if used, a guarantee of results. It is the way we express our political views. It is the way we hold our leaders and governments accountable. It is the way we bridge the gap between what we want our nation to be and what it is.

But when will the majority of women voters of our country exercise their most fundamental political right? Can you imagine what any of the Declaration signers would say if they learned how many women fail to vote in elections? They would be amazed and outraged. They would agree with a poster I saw in 1996. On it, there is a picture of a woman with a piece of tape covering her mouth and under it, it says, "Most politicians think women should be seen and not heard. In the last election, 54 million women agreed with them."

One hundred and fifty years ago, the women at Seneca Falls were silenced by someone else. Today, women, we silence ourselves. We have a choice. We have a voice. And if we are going to finish the work begun here, we must exercise our right to vote in every election we are eligible to vote in.

Looking to the Future

Much of who women are and what women do today can be traced to the courage, vision, and dedication of the pioneers who came together at Seneca Falls. Now it is our responsibility to finish the work they began. Let's ask ourselves, at the 200th anniversary of Seneca Falls, will they say that today's gathering also was a catalyst for action? Will they say that businesses, labor, religious organizations, the media, foundations, educators, every citizen in our society came to see the unfinished struggle of today as their struggle?

Will they say that we joined across lines of race and class, that we raised up those too often pushed down, and ultimately found strength in each other's differences and resolve in our common cause? Will we, like the champions at Seneca Falls, recognize that men must play a central role in this fight? How can we ever forget the impassioned plea of Frederick Douglass, issued in our defense of the right to vote?

How can we ever forget that young legislator from Tennessee by the name of Harry Burns, who was the deciding vote in ratifying the 19th Amendment. He was planning on voting "no," but then he got a letter from his mother with a simple message. The letter said, "Be a good boy, Harry, and do the right thing." And he did! Tennessee became the last state to ratify, proving that you can never, ever overestimate the power of one person to alter the course of history, or the power of a little motherly advice.

Will we look back and see that we have finally joined the rest of the advanced economies by creating systems of education, employment, child care, and healthcare that support and strengthen families and give all women real choices in their lives?

At the 200th anniversary celebration, will they say that women today supported each other in the choices we make? Will we admit once and for all there is no single cookie-cutter model for being a successful and fulfilled woman today, that we have so many choices? We can choose full-time motherhood or no family at all, or like most of us, seek to strike a balance between our family and our work, always trying to do what is right in our lives. Will we leave our children a world where it is self-evident that all men and women, boys and girls, are created equal? These are some of the questions we can ask ourselves.

Help us imagine a future that keeps faith with the sentiments expressed here in 1848. The future, like the past and the present, will not and cannot be perfect. Our daughters and granddaughters will face new challenges which we today cannot even imagine. But each of us can help prepare for that future by doing what we can to speak out for justice and equality for women's rights and human rights, to be on the right side of history, no matter the risk or cost, knowing that eventually the sentiments we express and the causes we advocate will succeed because they are rooted in the conviction that all people are entitled by their creator and by the promise of America to the freedom, rights, responsibilities, and opportunity of full citizenship. That is what I imagine for the future. I invite you to imagine with me and then to work together to make that future a reality.

CHAPTER 2

WOMEN AND THE WORKPLACE

EQUAL PAY FOR EQUAL WORK

Naomi Barko

On average, women earn 74 cents for every dollar earned by men. In the following article, Naomi Barko discusses the reasons for this pay gap. Jobs that are traditionally considered "women's work" consistently pay salaries that are lower than comparable "men's work," the author finds. One way of combating this disparity, she explains, is through comparable worth laws, which mandate that workers with equivalent skills, education, and experience be paid similar amounts. Barko reports that state legislatures are beginning to introduce bills establishing equal pay for public and private sector jobs. Nevertheless, objections to equal pay laws remain: Many businesses and conservative groups are opposed to raising women's wages, Barko writes, claiming men will not take jobs where their salaries are linked to women's pay. Barko is a freelance journalist who frequently writes about women's issues.

Hazel Dews is slightly embarrassed when you ask about her salary. She pauses and then confesses that after 25 years cleaning the Russell Senate Office Building in Washington five nights a week, she makes barely $22,000 a year. That's not what really bothers her, though. What irks her is that men who do the same job earn $30,000.

The men, she explains, are called "laborers." They can progress five grades. The women, however, are called "custodial workers," which means they can only advance two grades. "But," she protests, "they scrub with a mop and bucket. We scrub with a mop and bucket. They vacuum. We vacuum. They push a trash truck. We push a trash truck. The only thing they do that we don't is run a scrub machine. But that's on wheels, so we could do it too."

Women Consistently Earn Less Than Men

Thirty-seven years after the Equal Pay Act of 1963, American women working full time still earn an average of 74 cents for each dollar earned by men, according to a 2000 report published jointly by the 2000 American Federation of Labor and Congress of Industrial Organizations (AFL-CIO) and the Institute for Women's Policy Research (IWPR) in Washington. This affects all economic classes, but its impact is strongest on lower-income workers: If men and women were paid equally, more than 50 percent of low-income households across the country—dual-earner as well as single-mother—would rise above the poverty line.

New figures challenge the long-heard arguments that women's lower pay results from fewer years in the work force or time out for childbearing and rearing. The Women's Bureau of the Department of Labor cites a study by the president's Council of Economic Advisers showing that even in light of the vicissitudes of motherhood, 43 percent of the wage gap remains "unexplained," evidently due in large part to discrimination.

The Overview of Salary Surveys, published in 1999 by the National Committee on Pay Equity (NCPE), summarized 23 surveys of specific salary titles conducted by professional associations and trade magazines. It reported that, for instance, among women engineers—where the salary gap averages 26 percent—women with the same qualifications continue to earn less than men even after they've been in the field for many years (20.4 percent less among women with a B.S. degree and 20–24 years of experience; 19.2 percent less among women with an M.S. and 20–24 years experience). Yet another study found that women physicians earned less than men in 44 of 45 specialties, including obstetrics-gynecology (14 percent less) and pediatrics (15.8 percent less), with lower compensation only partly explainable by hours worked or time spent in the field. And a 1999 report by the American Association of University Professors found that though women had grown from 23 to 34 percent of faculty since 1975, the salary gap had actually widened in that time period.

But the biggest reason for the pay gap is not discrimination against individual women but rather discrimination against women's occupations. As the percentage of women in an occupation rises, wages tend to fall. More than 55 percent of employed women work in traditional "women's jobs"—librarians, clerical workers, nurses, teachers, and child care workers. If these women are compared not to male workers, but to women with similar education and experience in more gender-balanced occupations, they would earn about 18 percent—or $3,446— more per year, according to the IWPR. (The 8.5 percent of men in these jobs earn an average of $6,259 less per year than men of comparable backgrounds working in "men's" fields.)

Are Women's Jobs Worth Less?

Why are "women's jobs" less lucrative? Is a truck driver—who earns an average annual wage of $25,030—really 45 percent more valuable than a child care worker who may have a four-year degree in early childhood education? Is a beginning engineer really worth between

30 and 70 percent more than a beginning teacher? Rarely, in the almost daily reports of teacher shortages, is it mentioned that the market alone cannot account for the striking disparity between teachers' and other professionals' salaries. No one ever suggests that it might have something to do with the fact that 75 percent of elementary and secondary schoolteachers are women.

In response to these disparities, women are beginning to mobilize. In 1997, for example, Hazel Dews and 300 of her fellow women custodians joined the American Federation of State, County and Municipal Employees (AFSCME), which, after several futile attempts to negotiate, is now suing Dews's employer, the Architect of the Capitol, for equal pay. Since 1997, as women's membership in the labor movement has mushroomed to 40 percent, the AFL-CIO has conducted two surveys to discover the chief concerns of both union and nonunion working women. "And the runaway answer was equal pay," reports Karen Nussbaum, the director of the AFL-CIO's working women's department. Ninety-four percent of women in both surveys said equal pay was a top concern, and one-third—one-half of African-American women—said they did not have equal pay in their own jobs.

In 1999, calling pay equity a "family issue," the labor movement helped launch equal-pay bills in both houses of Congress and 27 state legislatures. Also in 1999, as Dews and her coworkers were demonstrating at the Capitol, the Eastman Kodak Company was agreeing to pay $13 million in present and retroactive wages to employees underpaid on the basis of either race or gender. The Massachusetts Institute of Technology, after protests by women faculty, made an unprecedented admission that it had discriminated against women "in salaries, space, awards, resources and response to outside offers."

Moreover, since 1997 the Office of Federal Contract Compliance Programs (OFCCP) has collected $10 million in equal-pay settlements from such corporations as Texaco, US Airways, Pepsi-Cola, the computer manufacturer Gateway, and health insurer Highmark, Inc. At the same time, two major national chains, the Home Depot and Publix Supermarkets, agreed to pay more than $80 million each to settle lawsuits based on sex discrimination.

Comparable Worth

Recently, advocates have arrived at what they believe to be an effective means of generating pay the equity—concept of "comparable worth," which, as the name suggests, requires two people with comparable skills, education, and experience to be paid comparable amounts, even when they're working at two very different jobs. The Xerox Corporation, for example, uses comparable worth analysis, weighing such factors as education, experience, skill, responsibility, decision making, and discomfort or danger in working conditions, to set salary levels within the country. During the 1980s, some 20 state governments studied the comparable worth of their own employees and made adjustments totaling almost $750 million in increased pay to women. Minnesota, the leader in the field, has made pay equity adjustments in 1,544 counties and localities.

Perhaps the most dramatic argument for comparable worth, however, was made by a man. In the class action suit *AFSCME* v. *Washington State* in 1982, one of the nine named plaintiffs was Milt Tedrow, a licensed practical nurse at Eastern State Hospital in Spokane. Approaching retirement and realizing that his "woman's" job wouldn't give him much of a pension, Tedrow switched to carpentry at the same hospital. To qualify as an LPN he had needed at least four years of experience, four quarters of schooling, and a license. As a carpenter, he was self-taught, had no paid work experience, and had no need of a license. And yet when he transferred from the top of the LPN wage scale to the bottom of the carpenter's, his salary jumped more than $200 a month—from $1,614 to $1,826. Why, Tedrow wondered at the time, does the state resent "paying people decently who are taking care of people's bodies, when they'd pay a lot for someone fixing cars or plumbing?"

Since then, the courts have ruled that evidence of unfair salaries is not enough to prove violation of the Equal Pay Act. Plaintiffs must prove that employers intentionally discriminated by lowering women's wages in comparison to men's. But some unions have prevailed on comparable worth questions by way of negotiations.

Service Employees International Union Local 715, for example, in Santa Clara County, just south of San Francisco, won nearly $30 million for 4,500 county employees, from secretaries to mental-health counselors. A study of some 150 job titles, performed by a consulting firm chosen jointly by the county and the union, showed that underpayment was common in job classes with more than 50 percent minorities, such as licensed vocational nurses and beginning social workers, and that 70 percent of such positions were filled by women. "We worked for at least three years to bring our male members along on this," says Kristy Sermersheim, Local 715's executive secretary. "When the county argued that in order to raise women's wages they'd have to lower men's, we refused to even discuss it. We kept regular pay negotiations completely separate."

Another key to the local's success was the staunch support of allies among local women's groups. "We had 54 women's community groups on our side," reports Sermersheim. "The National Organization for Women, the American Association of University Women, the League of Women Voters, the Silicon Valley women engineers. . . ." On the day the county board of supervisors voted on whether to proceed with the study, the local delivered 1,000 pink balloons—symbolizing the pink-collar ghetto—to workplaces around the city. "We had balloons everywhere" recalls Sermersheim, "We had Unitarian women out there singing 'Union Maid.'"

Pushing Equal Pay

It is this kind of coalition that pay equity advocates are counting on to push through the equal-pay bills now before state legislatures. Many of the new bills, unlike those passed in the 1980s, would extend comparable worth to private as well as public employees and would specifically extend benefits to minorities. Most are based on the fair pay act designed in consultation with the NCPE—a coalition of 30 women's, labor, civil rights, and religious groups—and introduced in Congress in 1999 by two Democrats, Senator Tom Harkin of Iowa and Representative Eleanor Holmes Norton of the District of Columbia. . . .

So far the new state bills have met with only modest success. The New Jersey and New Mexico legislatures have voted to study pay equity in both public and private employment, and Vermont's legislature voted to study just state employment. In Maine, where the new welfare laws gave rise to a commission to study poverty among working parents, it was discovered that the state already had a 1965 law on the books that mandated equal pay for both public and private employees and that specifically mentioned comparable worth. The state is now studying ways to put the law into effect.

Objections to Equal Pay

Efforts like these have raised opposition from business and conservative groups. Economist Diana Furchtgott-Roth, a resident fellow at the American Enterprise Institute who has represented business at an NCPE forum, supports "equal pay for equal work" but claims that comparable worth causes labor shortages because men refuse to take jobs where their wages will be tied to women's. "How can a government bureaucrat calculate if a secretary is worth the same as a truck driver, or a nurse as an oil-driller?"

In Ontario, Canada, Furchtgott-Roth says, where the practice of comparable worth is more common, day care centers are actually closing down because parents can't afford to pay for the higher salaries. But these charges turn out to be only partially true. Child care centers in Ontario were threatened when a Progressive Conservative government succeeded the liberal New Democrats and slashed funding. But the centers have not closed down. After a court challenge and an enormous public outcry, the provincial government is still subsidizing pay equity for child care workers (who, even with subsidies, earn an average of only $16,000 a year).

State employment officials in Minnesota and Wisconsin, two states with comparable worth laws, say that any labor shortages have far more to do with the tight labor market than with comparable worth. "There's a lot of flexibility in the law," says Faith Zwemke, Minnesota's pay equity coordinator. "For information technology people, for instance, we can give them signing bonuses and let them advance faster within the parameters of the policy."

Some male workers inevitably do resent women getting increases. "But many men can see pay equity as a family issue," says Karen Nussbaum of the AFL-CIO. A poll by Democratic pollster Celinda Lake showed that six out of 10 voters, both men and women, said equal pay was good for families.

Pay equity advocates had better be patient and persistent. The market has been biased against women at least since it was written in the Old Testament that when a vow offering is made to God, it should be based on the value of the person, and "[if] a male, from the age of twenty years up to the age of sixty years, your assessment shall be fifty silver shekels . . . and if it is a female, your assessment shall be thirty shekels." At this rate, winning equal pay may take a long time.

THE GLASS CEILING: LIMITS ON WOMEN'S ADVANCEMENT

Barbara Beck

In many developed countries, although women make up half of the workforce, their representation in top-level executive positions typically ranges from only 1 to 10 percent, reports Barbara Beck. She explains that women's progress up the corporate ladder is often hampered by the "glass ceiling," an invisible barrier created by prejudices against women in the workplace. Women are frequently perceived as less committed to their careers than men, she writes, and they find it difficult to break into the male-dominated corporate culture. Beck explores how this issue is being addressed in the United States and other developed nations, examining the progress that is being made in removing the obstacles to women's advancement and in acknowledging the worth of the unique qualities and experiences that women bring to the workplace. Beck is a writer for the *Economist*, a British magazine.

It's always lonely at the top, but if you are a woman it can be utterly desolate. Whether in politics, business, the professions or academia, the top layer everywhere is almost exclusively male. This may not come as a surprise in countries where few women work, but it is also largely true, and more baffling, in America and Europe's Nordic region, where nearly half the labour force is female.

There does not seem to be much of a correlation between a reasonable number of women in, say, politics and a reasonable number of women in, say, high-level management posts. In Germany, for example, over a quarter of all Members of Parliament (MPs) are women, but a survey of the 70,000 largest companies showed that women's share of top executive and board positions was only 1–3%. In America, which is generally thought to be a decade or more ahead of Europe on such matters, women hold about 10% of the board seats of Fortune 500 companies—still low, but better than it was; whereas in the House of Representatives women have a share of only 12.6% and in the Senate just 9%, way below the figures in many European countries.

Women in politics have come a surprisingly long way in a short time. At the beginning of the twentieth century few countries had universal suffrage for men, let alone women. By the early 1920s America, Germany and the Nordic countries, among others, had introduced votes for all adult women, and Britain followed in 1928. But France and Italy waited until 1944 and 1945 respectively, Greece until 1952 and Portugal, amazingly, until 1976.

Only the Nordic countries have got anywhere near parity in the number of women MPs. They also have the highest proportion of women in government, with women ministers making up between a third and half the total. But even in the progressive north, more often than not the women get the "soft" jobs such as health, education, labour, social affairs and culture. The heavyweight portfolios such as foreign affairs, finance and justice almost invariably go to men. Finland is the only country where at some point every single portfolio has been held by a woman. Women prime ministers such as Britain's Margaret Thatcher remain as rare as hen's teeth.

Looking for Women in Business

The hope must be that the example of women in top political posts will eventually rub off on the business world, but for the moment there is little sign of it. In Britain, for instance, only one Financial Times Stock Exchange (FTSE) 100 company is headed by a woman: Marjorie Scardino, the (American) chief executive of Pearson (which owns half of *The Economist*). And even in the Nordic countries, where women are well represented in politics and the public sector, they are conspicuously absent from higher management.

One notable exception is Antonia Ax:son Johnson, chief executive of Sweden's Axel Johnson Group, a retailing, wholesaling and food multinational that employs 18,000 people. Ms Ax:son Johnson concedes that attitudes and expectations in senior business circles remain deeply traditional. Within her own organisation she has tried hard to give women a chance, doubling their share in middle management from 20% to 40%, but says it is not always easy. Ms Ax:son Johnson herself is clearly a highly effective manager who seems to have had no trouble combining four children with a demanding career. But she had the enormous advantage of working for the family firm, which she took over from her father.

Across the Atlantic, an annual survey of Fortune 500 companies conducted by Catalyst, a New York–based research organisation that works with an impressive list of member companies to promote women in business, has noted that more of them are getting into senior positions. Even so, in 1997 they still accounted for only 3% of jobs at the very top of those companies (defined as chief executive, president, chairman and their immediate deputies). Immediately below that level the picture looks brighter: in 1998, 419 of the Fortune 500 had at least one woman on the board, and a third of them two or more.

The biggest companies are far better at promoting women than those at the bottom end of the Fortune 500. And as you might expect, women directors are much more likely to pop up in industries such as cosmetics, food services, airlines and computer software than in, say, engineering or construction.

Obstacles to Progress

What is stopping women from getting right to the top? According to Sheila Wellington, Catalyst's president, that depends on whom you ask. Male managers will say that women are so new to the upper reaches of corporate life that there are simply not enough of them in the pipeline. Even more important, where women have made it to senior positions, it has usually been in support functions such as human resources, public affairs and certain kinds of finance jobs. Few of them have had experience of line positions where they have had profit-and-loss responsibilities, say as a plant manager or head of sales and marketing. Yet it is precisely in these line positions that managers gather the experience they need to propel them to the top.

Ask the women themselves, and they will agree that they are handicapped by lack of general management experience. But they will also point to a raft of other obstacles, especially male myths and preconceptions. Men suspect women of being less committed to their careers, unwilling to work long hours, lacking the right training and skills, and not assertive enough—or, conversely, too aggressive. Women also feel excluded from informal networks, and often find the corporate culture hostile. Unlike men, they rarely have mentors within the organisation to give them advice. Sooner or later they hit the "glass ceiling", that infamous invisible barrier created by individual and organisational prejudices.

How many of them really want to break through? Plenty of men mischievously suggest that few women are prepared to put in decades of 70-hour weeks and endless travel to get to the top. Quite a few women would agree that there is no way they could put in those hours and still do their second shift at home. But, they say, there should be no need to: if work were organised more rationally, those long hours should not be necessary. Whatever the reasons, many women do not even try for the top jobs. For men, one of the classic entry routes to the executive suite is via business school and an MBA. But at the top business schools in America, women MBA students on average make up less than 30% of the total.

Patricia O'Brien, dean of the Simmons Graduate School of Management in Boston, says that women need special training to learn how to make it in a male-dominated corporate world. Her college is the only business school in the world designed exclusively for women. It has compiled its own dossier of 150 case studies in which top female executives figure prominently, providing Ms O'Brien's students with "a mental Rolodex of role models" (one of the things ambitious women say they particularly lack). Over the past 20 years her college has released some 3,000 female graduates into the corporate world, many of whom now have high-powered jobs in Fortune 500 companies. But, she points out wistfully, the proportion of women in top management in America has stayed at around 2% for the past 40 years.

Pipeline Dreams

What has changed dramatically, she says, is the proportion of women in middle management, which over the same period has risen from perhaps 4% to 40% of the total: surely a sign that the much-quoted pipeline is at last beginning to fill up. America's Glass Ceiling Commission, a government-appointed body set up in 1991 to investigate where women got stuck, came to similar conclusions. Europe is moving the same way, but remains further behind. A survey of the European Union's (EU) banking industry, by Sigrid Quack of the Social Science Centre in Berlin, found that women on average made up about half the total staff of the banks studied, but only a little over a quarter even of lower management. And their average share of the top jobs was only 8%. Even at Marks and Spencer, a large British retailer noted for its enlightened policies, the female ranks thin markedly towards the top. Women's share of the company's total staff is 85%; of its managers, 60%; of its senior managers, 30%; and of its executive directors, just one.

Prescriptions for women trying to crash through the glass ceiling are much the same everywhere: get experience in line management; develop your skills and self-confidence; find yourself a mentor within the organisation who will smooth your path; get supervisors and senior management on your side; and above all, make sure you work for a company that really believes in giving women a chance.

The only way to get companies truly interested in promoting women is to convince them that it is good for their business. In essence, the argument runs something like this. First, women make up about half of mankind; there is no evidence that the raw material of intelligence, energy and other qualities that make people perform well in jobs is unevenly distributed between the sexes; moreover, women in rich countries are now generally as well-educated as men, so are able to offer similar qualifications. If you are recruiting only men, you are therefore narrowing your choice to only half the brightest and best people.

Second, if you are already employing women and have invested in adapting their skills to your particular needs, it makes economic sense to accommodate them by offering, say, maternity leave or flexible hours, rather than risk losing them and having to start all over again with someone else. Sainsbury, a large British retailer, reckons that replacing a fully trained first-line supervisor costs about £10,000

($16,500) a time. The more highly trained the employee, the more expensive she becomes to replace. Keeping staff turnover down can save a lot of money.

Third, women can benefit the business by bringing a different approach to an issue. This is not the same as saying that women have a distinctive management style, about which there has been much fuzzy talk. They may or may not be more intuitive, more people-oriented and better suited to today's flatter hierarchies than men. In truth, though, how they manage will depend far more on the organisation and the task in hand than on their gender. The only consistent difference in style researchers have been able to pinpoint is that women managers are more likely to listen to other people.

Dare to Be Different

But women undoubtedly have a different experience of life from men, may ask different questions and are seen as different by outsiders. All these qualities contribute to diversity in the workforce, a newly fashionable concept that refers not just to women but also to every conceivable kind of minority. One of its many advocates is the Conference Board, a research organisation with a worldwide membership of 2,800 companies, including many household names. It takes diversity so seriously that it organises an annual conference to promote the cause. At 1998's bash in New York, you could have listened to Jack Smith, head of General Motors, explaining why he believes diversity is critical to the success of organisations, and a host of diversity directors from companies such as IBM, Procter & Gamble and Quaker Oats wondering whether there was enough of it about.

Terence McGuire, seconded from accountants Pricewaterhouse-Coopers to the Conference Board's Workforce Diversity Group, insists that diversity makes sound business sense. For example, the teams his own firm fields for a client engagement are increasingly expected to match client companies' own diverse workforces, which means that sending in the standard consignment of white males may no longer be appropriate. American consumers and shareholders, too, are becoming more diverse, and expect that fact to be reflected in the companies they deal with. As companies become more global, they need a more heterogeneous labour force that is sensitive to social, economic, political and cultural differences. The potential benefits of diversity, say its champions, include better employee morale, less absenteeism, improved client relations and new ideas for top management. The trouble is that many diversity programmes are so new that as yet there is little hard evidence of their beneficial effect on the bottom line.

Women Working for Themselves

Until such evidence is forthcoming, many senior managers will remain sceptical, and many women will continue to bang their heads against the glass ceiling. But more and more of them are deciding that their heads would be better employed on something more constructive: becoming entrepreneurs. In America, women are setting up new businesses at twice the rate of men. From dress shop to design studio to software house, they are realising their dreams. According to America's National Foundation for Women Business Owners, the number of women-owned enterprises is about 8 million, or nearly 40% of the total. Britain has also seen lively growth in this area, although in continental Europe and Japan progress has been more halting. Both the Organization for Economic Cooperation and Development (OECD) and the EU are trying to encourage women entrepreneurs through a variety of support and training programmes, not least because they see self-employment as a way of reducing joblessness.

Setting up a business is not necessarily the road to riches. An analysis of American household income figures by the Institute for Women's Policy Research, a Washington think-tank, found that full-time self-employed women earn only half as much per hour, on average, as full-time female employees. Moreover, a large majority of women entrepreneurs work less than full-time, so for many women, the analysis concluded, "self-employment does not appear to be a feasible method of supporting a family by itself."

Still, for frustrated female managers, it is a chance of realising an exciting business idea, and sometimes it comes off. The other great attraction is that entrepreneurs, at least in theory, get to set their own hours. Compared with the rigidity of corporate life, the flexibility of self-employment seems to offer a solution to many working women's biggest problem: reconciling career and family.

THE MYTH OF THE GLASS CEILING

Diana Furchtgott-Roth

Statistics seem to show that very few women are able to break through the "glass ceiling" that keeps them from advancing in their careers as high as men do. However, Diana Furchtgott-Roth contends, the glass ceiling is actually a myth constructed by feminists. Feminists want women to have special privileges such as affirmative action, she writes, so they manipulate statistics to make it look as if women face job and wage discrimination. The reality, Furchtgott-Roth reports, is that women are actually closing the employment gender gap, earning more advanced degrees than ever before and gaining the experience needed for top-level management jobs. Nevertheless, Furchtgott-Roth maintains that the ratio of men to women in top positions will never be equal because many women choose to spend more time raising a family than concentrating on their career path. Furchtgott-Roth is the coauthor of *The Feminist Dilemma: When Success Is Not Enough.*

It has become fashionable to talk about a glass ceiling for women, an invisible career barrier which cannot be overcome by hardworking females with even the most impeccable qualifications. It's a sad story of women who work shoulder to shoulder with men and then, just as that chief executive officer job comes into view . . . presto!, the glass barrier descends. The men move up, the women are left behind.

The glass ceiling was given the seal of credibility with the federal Glass Ceiling Commission in 1991, which put out a ponderous report authenticating these claims. And other institutions, most recently the New York firm Catalyst, periodically release studies showing that women make up only a small fraction of corporate officers at the nation's largest companies. The conclusion of all these studies, of course, is that life is unfair to women, who need special affirmative-action programs to progress in the workplace.

The Glass Ceiling Is a Feminist Fantasy

But is this sad story true, or is it just the fantasy of a group of whiny females for whom the tale of the glass ceiling is a convenient way of advancing their own interests? In fact, the glass ceiling is a figment of feminist imaginations, up there with the myths of alar poisoning, and Jews eating Christian babies on Passover. Why was this tale concocted? The answer is obvious: It's in the interests of feminists to portray women as victims, since it gives women greater economic benefits. Who wouldn't want preferred access to government contracts, promotion of less-qualified members of their group over others and a whole apparatus set up to ensure proper representation of their relevant group? As a woman professional, I should be delighted, except that it imposes substantial economic costs on society as a whole, shared by all consumers and taxpayers.

Efforts in corporations, universities and governments to counteract the so-called glass ceiling in the name of equality rely on a whole cadre of "diversity specialists" whose role is to ensure equal representation of various groups in different professions. Corporations hold sensitivity training rather than computer training and promote the less-qualified to managerial positions to be "fair." Universities have quotas for female faculty and governments have minority set-asides.

All of this costs money, reduces efficiency and results in higher prices for corporations' products, higher tuition costs at universities and higher taxes for individuals. Economic growth is slowed, reducing job creation—the most important avenue for everyone's advancement. Yes, some women win—but everyone else pays for it.

Just consider some facts: Today women are well-represented in the professions; they continue to enter fields of study previously dominated by men; they are starting their own businesses in record numbers; and they are winning elective office throughout the country. Laws barring discrimination against women are on the books and enforced. All those gains clearly contradict the image of women as victims struggling against discrimination in the workplace.

Women Are Catching Up to Men

Since 1982 women have earned more than 50 percent of all bachelor's degrees and all master's degrees, and in other fields women are closing the gap fast. Whereas 2 or 3 percent of all law degrees awarded went to women in the fifties and sixties and 5 percent in 1970, women now earn about 43 percent of those degrees. Fewer than 1 percent of dentistry degrees were awarded to women in the fifties, sixties and seventies, yet women now receive 38 percent of these degrees. Similar trends hold for doctoral and medical degrees. In 1996 women represented 54 percent of the class admitted to Yale Medical School.

As they move into previously male-dominated fields, women's wages have been steadily rising relative to men's wages. It is true that, on average, women earn less than men, when all women's wages are averaged with all men's wages. But that is because these averages compare people who have different educational backgrounds and who have chosen different jobs and different hours. When comparing wages, like should be compared to like, not nurses to engineers.

In studies accounting for demographic and job characteristics such as education, race, age, part- or full-time employment, public- or private-sector status, occupation and union or nonunion status, women earn almost as much as men. The National Longitudinal Survey of Youth found that, among people ages 27 to 33 who never have had a child, women's earnings are close to 98 percent of men's. A study of economics and engineering doctorates by June O'Neill came up with similar results. However, many women choose occupations and careers that allow them more flexibility in work hours, and these positions typically pay less.

Furthermore, the wage gap widens once women have children, presumably since the children place additional demands on these women's time.

The most outstanding gains made by women lately have been in the business world. In 1972 there were only 400,000 women-owned businesses. Today there are approximately 8 million such businesses in the United States, employing 15.5 million people and generating $1.4 trillion in sales. The number of women-owned businesses increased 43 percent from 1987 to 1992. Women are starting businesses at twice the rate of men.

Why Are So Few Women at the Top?

With all this progress, why did the Glass Ceiling Commission conclude that only 5 percent of senior managers at Fortune 2000 companies are women, leading to charges of glass ceilings and discrimination? Because the commission used a statistically corrupt methodology to prove its point and further its agenda. Rather than comparing the number of women qualified to hold top positions with those who actually hold those jobs, it compared the number of women in the labor force, without reference to experience or education levels, with those wielding power at top corporations. This resulted in a politically useful low number of 5 percent.

The real answer is that there are comparatively few educated and experienced women available to be nominated for such high-level positions. Typical qualifications for top management positions include both a master's degree in business administration and 25 years of work experience, and there aren't many such women around. Look at the data: Women received less than 5 percent of graduate degrees in the sixties and seventies, and these are the graduates who now are at the pinnacle of their professions. That supports the "pipeline" theory, which holds that women have not reached the top in greater numbers because they have not been "in the pipeline" long enough.

Moreover, to reach the CEO level, individuals have to be committed to their jobs and work 60-hour weeks continuously throughout their career. Many men and many women, especially mothers, do not want to do this. Moving in and out of the workforce in accordance with family demands is not conducive to being a CEO of a major corporation. Yet many mothers do interrupt their careers in just this fashion, since these mothers believe that they are the best caregivers for their children.

There is nothing wrong with choosing a career which allows more time at home with less pay rather than one with more time at work with more pay, and in either case women should not be considered victims of a glass ceiling and in need of government intervention such as affirmative action. One consequence of those choices, however, is that out of the relatively small group of women who have the educational requirements and training to be CEOs—those who got their graduate degrees in the sixties—fewer have put in the 25 years of 60-hour weeks that a CEO position requires. The result is a small pool of qualified women for those kinds of positions.

The good news is that in the future more women will be getting the necessary educational qualifications and more of those who graduated in the seventies and later will be moving into corporate positions, so the trend toward increasing numbers of female corporate executives will continue. However, because of the unique position that mothers play in rearing children, the ratio of male to female CEOs is unlikely to reach 50-50. This is not necessarily bad. The important point is that women should be free to choose their career paths.

Women Do Not Need Special Treatment

Now, if outcomes at the CEO level are not likely to be 50-50 on their own, does that show that women face a glass ceiling? Not at all: The data make it clear that women now have equality of opportunity and that those who choose to rise to high positions in corporations can do so. Cultural barriers to women in top positions largely have disappeared—just ask Secretary of State Madeleine Albright. When discrimination does occur, there are legal remedies to deal with it under the Civil Rights Act and the Equal Pay Act. Women are bringing these cases to court and winning.

Whereas the glass-ceiling myth benefits women in the short run, its effects well could backfire against women over the long term. With special preferences for women in the workplace, the achievements of all women can be called into question, since it can be assumed that progress has been made because of quotas and preferences rather than ability. When Albright's selection was announced, there was some speculation that President Bill Clinton had chosen her because of her sex rather than because of her preeminent qualifications. Albright was confirmed by the Senate irrespective of these doubts. But the patients shopping for heart surgeons or the retirees looking for financial planners well may prefer to put their lives and their money into male hands, even though the particular female heart surgeons and financial planners under consideration may not have benefited from affirmative action.

Some say that women in America face a glass ceiling: that they are paid less than men; that they cannot reach the highest rungs of the corporate ladder; that they cannot enter any profession they choose; that they would benefit from more government intervention in the marketplace; and that they need affirmative action and quotas. But none of these is true. These views are being advanced because it is in feminists' interests for women to have preferential treatment and to have all consumers and taxpayers pay for it. It's a great scam—and they're getting away with it.

WOMEN IN THE SCIENCES

Ziauddin Sardar

In the following article, cultural critic and scholar Ziauddin Sardar discusses why women are underrepresented and discriminated against in scientific fields. This discrimination begins in school, he explains, where girls are not usually encouraged to pursue scientific work. Women who do become scientists are consistently undervalued, he maintains, and must struggle for both jobs and recognition. Sardar reports that female scientists often earn less than their male counterparts and have a harder time securing laboratory space and project funding. Feminist scholars blame these problems on a historical male bias in science, he notes; they argue that scientific research into such subjects as biology and evolution is often grounded in a masculine perspective or influenced by traditional gender stereotypes. According to the author, these scholars propose that scientists should strive to include varying perspectives in their research and work toward a fairer representation of women in scientific fields. Sardar is editor of the journal *Futures*.

Professor Susan Greenfield, the director of the Royal Institution, is the 122nd most powerful person in Britain. This surprising revelation was made in the recently published Channel 4/Observer Power 300 list. Greenfield is a highly respected neuroscientist and, given her media profile, I have no reason to dispute the claim. But the discovery—if I can describe it as such—is surprising because she is, well, not just a scientist but also a woman.

Women scientists are not normally known for their power and influence. Indeed, women scientists are conspicuous largely by their absence in positions of power and influence in science. Worse: women are just rare in science.

Why? One obvious answer is that women are discriminated against. The discrimination starts in schools where girls are slotted into subjects that are seen as their "natural" province. It continues to adolescence and adulthood, with the result that women are systematically

Excerpted from "A Male Preserve," by Ziauddin Sardar, *New Statesman*, November 15, 1999. Copyright © 1999 by New Statesman, Ltd. Reprinted with permission.

discouraged from engaging in the kinds of thinking necessary for skills in scientific, mathematical and engineering work.

Female Scientists Are Undervalued

Those women who do get into scientific careers are contained within demarcated boundaries. They are trapped in a pattern of segregated employment and under-recognition from which few can escape. Numerous studies and reports have shown that women scientists are mainly to be found in the lower echelons of the scientific enterprise, and the achievements of the few who can find the resources to carry out independent research are systematically undervalued relative to similar achievements by men.

The most recent report comes from the Massachusetts Institute of Technology (MIT). It is the product of a two-year battle between Nancy Hopkins, a molecular biologist, and the MIT establishment. Hopkins joined MIT in 1973 and became a tenured professor in 1982. Her work was constantly hampered by a system stacked against women scientists. She discovered that her problems were common to other women scientists at MIT. They often got the worst jobs, earned less and had less prestige within their departments. There were only 15 tenured women, compared with 197 men. While male scientists were getting whole new buildings, women were confined to ridiculously small laboratory spaces—some could not even get a closet. Women had more teaching responsibilities than their male colleagues, but faced more difficulty in obtaining grants.

Hopkins compared the science environment at the Institute to "a Wild West culture where the strong take from the weak". She organised other women at MIT and ended up chairing a committee that published a report, in April 1999, on sexual prejudice there. Hopkins's report is seen as a milestone: for the first time, a prestigious institution such as MIT publicly acknowledged a "long-standing pattern of gender bias".

Of course, the long-standing pattern is not confined to MIT. It is a standard feature of science. Even the European Commission now accepts that discrimination against women in science is widespread. In 1999, it established a "network of networks" of women in science as a pressure group to expose sexual prejudice and campaign for more women in science.

Science Is Gender Biased

Is sexual prejudice merely a question of management of science, or is there something inherent in science itself that discriminates against women? Feminist scholars of science have been arguing for a few decades now that science itself is inherently anti-women. At one level, it is simply the content of science that appals many women. As Sandra Harding, professor of philosophy at the University of Delaware

and author of the influential *Science Questions in Feminism*, puts it:
how many women will choose a career goal of building a bomb, tor-
turing animals or manufacturing machines that put one's sisters out
of work? But the feminist analysis goes much deeper and points a fin-
ger at the nature of science itself.

Feminist scholars accuse science of being inherently "androcen-
tric". Consider, for example, the traditional evolutionary theories that
tell us the roots of some human behaviour are said to be found in the
history of human evolution. The origins of Western, middle-class
social life, where men go out to do what a man's got to do and
women tend the babies and look after the kitchen, are to be found in
the bonding of "man-the-hunter"; in the early phases of evolution,
women were the gatherers and men went out to bring in the beef.
These theories are based on the discovery of chipped stones that are
said to provide evidence for the male invention of tools for use in the
hunting and preparation of animals. However, if you look at the same
stones with different cultural perceptions, say one where women are
seen as the main providers of the group—and we know that such cultures exist even today—you can argue that these stones were used by
women to kill animals, cut corpses, dig up roots, break down seed
pods or hammer and soften tough roots to prepare them for consumption. You now have a totally different hypothesis, and the
course of evolutionary theory changes. Other developments in science, such as the rise of IQ tests, behavioural conditioning, foetal
research and socio-biology, can be analysed with similar logic.

Gender bias thus emerges in the way basic questions are asked in
science. The kind of data that is gathered and appealed to as evidence
for different types of questions enhances this bias further. Feminist
scholarship of science, which is truly monumental both in terms of
quality and quantity, has analysed almost every branch of science. It
has shown that the focus on quantitative measures, analysis of variation, impersonal and excessively abstract conceptual schemes, is both
a distinctively masculine tendency and also one that serves to hide its
own gendered character. And it has revealed that the prioritising of
mathematics and abstract thought, standards of objectivity, the construction of scientific method and the instrumental nature of scientific rationality, are all based on the notion of ideal masculinity.

Considering a Wider Perspective

Would a fair representation of women in science change anything? To
begin with, it would have obvious economic advantages. Knowledge-
based economies, in dire need of trained scientists, cannot afford to
squander half of their scientific potential. There is also the argument
that more women in science would open up science to a wider range
of material and social problems. For example, the problems of the
Third World would receive greater emphasis and more research sup-

port. But the feminist scholars are arguing for something more.

Sandra Harding has suggested that women would introduce a shift away from conventional scientific method and objectivity to what she calls "strong objectivity". Strong objectivity requires the scientists to take perspectives of the "outsiders"—the social scientists, the environmentalists, the housewife, the non-Western cultures—into their description and explanations of the subject of scientific inquiry. In a similar vein, Hilary Rose, one of our most respected feminist scholars, talks about "responsible rationality" that restores care and concern within scientific objectivity.

The argument here is not that feminist notions of science should be recognised as legitimate and desirable alongside the conventional practice of science. Or that anti-sexist concepts, theories, methods, and interpretations should be regarded as scientifically equal. Or even that more women should be trained and recruited to work alongside colleagues and within institutional norms and practices that are obviously discriminatory so that women could become men in order to practice science. The argument is that having a fairer representation of women in science will not actually solve the problem; science will continue to be discriminatory. Only a fundamental transformation of concepts, methods and interpretations in science will produce real change. Feminist scholars are asking for nothing less than a re-orientation of the logic of scientific discovery. I am wholeheartedly with them.

SEXUAL HARASSMENT IN THE WORKPLACE

Rachel Thompson

In the following selection, Rachel Thompson explains that many women experience sexual harassment in the workplace, including unwanted sexual advances, offensive comments, and sexually suggestive behaviors. Sexual harassment can seriously impact women's job performance by making them feel uncomfortable or threatened at work, she writes. Thompson notes that supervisors often overlook such harassment or are themselves perpetrators, which makes the problem more difficult to eradicate. On the other hand, she reports, many large corporations are taking a strong stand against sexual harassment, and unions are instituting procedures designed to eliminate harassment and protect victims. According to Thompson, experts agree that developing proactive policies for dealing with harassment is the best way to stop it. Thompson writes for *Herizons*, a Canadian feminist magazine.

Patricia Allen heard someone following her during her nightly patrol. She thought an inmate had escaped. Terrified, she informed her supervisors. Their response surprised her: it was just a co-worker playing a 'prank'.

Allen wasn't amused. It wasn't the first time her safety had been compromised by co-workers. At a conference of the Law Union of Ontario in 2001, Allen and other former guards broke their two-decade silence, describing acts of harassment that ranged from pornography strewn around the security office, to having their cars vandalized.

Sexual Harassment in Canada

Statistics vary, but between 40 and 70 percent of Canadian women and around five percent of men report that they have experienced sexual harassment, usually from supervisors. All provincial legislatures and Parliament have enacted human rights statutes that prohibit sex discrimination, including sexual harassment. In law, sexual harassment focusses on behaviours: unwanted physical contact, sexual advances, requests for sexual favours, suggestive or offensive comments or gestures emphasizing sexuality, sexual identity or sexual orientation.

Its effects are far reaching. According to Constance Backhouse and Leah Cohen, authors of *The Secret Oppression: Sexual Harassment of Working Women*, "Sexual harassment can manifest itself physically and psychologically. . . . It can poison a woman's work environment to the extent that her livelihood is in danger".

Allen says she was told that she would be put into a cell to deal with any trouble with an inmate and that her male co-workers would not help. Another former guard, Julie Blair, told delegates that, "I actually found cells left open from the previous shift." Blair and Allen were hired in 1980 as part of a Corrections Canada project to bring female guards into federal men's prisons. Six years later, both of them quit.

Canadian courts and tribunals have established that employers must provide employees with a harassment-free workplace. If they don't, they can face significant financial penalties. The most common type of compensation is monetary, for lost wages or salary and pain and humiliation. Sexual harassment awards as high as $50,000 have been ordered by human rights commissions. However, the costs of harassment to workplaces go beyond the financial. Harassment also takes a toll on lost productivity, damages the image of the workplace and damages the overall working environment for employees.

Sexual harassment is not restricted to any one field, as one Canadian study confirmed. According to a Conference Board of Canada's June 2001 report, one third of female senior executives left their last job because of sexual harassment.

"We're not talking nervous entry-level graduates. We're talking ambitious, talented women," said Barbara Orser, author of the report. The study involved 350 women with senior posts in the public and private sectors. Respondents were also asked to predict when women would achieve equal representation in 10 key areas. Close to half predicted that discrimination in the workplace will always exist.

"Clearly we have work to do," observed Pamela Jeffrey, founder of the Toronto-based Women's Executive Network that commissioned the poll. Even the most optimistic respondents predicted that it would be more than 30 years before sexual harassment is wiped out.

In 1987, the Supreme Court of Canada unanimously ruled that employers are liable for the discriminatory acts of their employees in the course of their employment. In doing so, it overturned a Federal Court of Appeal which had ruled earlier that, while Bonnie Robichaud had been sexually harassed by her supervisor at the department of National Defence, the department was not liable for the contravention of her rights. The Court ruled in *Robichaud* that the purpose of human rights legislation is to remove discrimination. As a result of the ruling, employers covered by the federal act are liable for the conduct of their employees.

Today, the Canadian military continues to see women leave en masse because of discrimination, harassment and sexual assault by their peers and supervisors. "Although increasing numbers of women are joining the navy, the attrition data indicates that a disproportionate number are leaving hard sea occupations," concluded a defence department review in 2000. This follows a 1988 *Maclean's* magazine investigation that revealed that cases of sexual assault in the military routinely went unpunished; an Armed Forces hotline was set up to register complaints.

A Serious Moral Problem

Sexual harassment is more than a discrimination issue, a liability issue, a communication problem, an employee-relations problem or a productivity problem. According to the book, *Sexual Harassment*, edited by philosophy professor Edmund Wall, sexual harassment represents a "serious moral problem."

Not according to Camille Paglia, who has published essays promoting the idea that women are harassed and physically abused by men due to natural forces. "Men," writes Paglia, the author of *Sex, Art, and American Culture*, "must quest, pursue, court or seize."

However, the fact that many men do not act this way speaks for itself, according to those who call sexual harassment a social, not a biological, problem.

"The idea is that biology cannot be questioned or changed, and is legitimate . . ." wrote Catharine A. McKinnon in her 1979 classic, *Sexual Harassment of Working Women: A Case of Sex Discrimination*. "In these cases, we are dealing with a male who is allegedly exercising his power as an employer, his power over a woman's material survival, and his sexual prerogatives as a man, to subject a woman sexually."

Ethicist Vaughana Macy Feary in her essay, "Sexual Harassment: Why the Corporate World Still Doesn't Get It," defends sexual harassment policies saying, "Even the most liberal moral theories acknowledge that harm to others is our strongest moral reason for restricting liberty." As Feary points out in "Sexual Harassment," "Biological drives can be restrained and cultures, including corporate cultures, can be changed."

Beverly Suek, a Winnipeg-based harassment investigator agrees. "It's not about sex, it's about power and the misuse and abuse of power, even when it's between colleagues."

Suek is not surprised that the Conference Board study participants were so pessimistic about the chances of eradicating sexual harassment from the workplace. "Thirty years ago you were told to either 'Put up or shut up,'" she says. Today she sees a growing lack of acceptance of harassment. "I think we can consciously change corporate culture from one that is harassing to one that is respectful."

Sharron Gould, president of the Manitoba Association for Respectful

Workplaces, concurs. "We're also seeing men verbalize their intolerance [for harassment] and when that happens, there is less harassment."

Harassment at the Top

One thing that researchers and human resource experts all agree on is that harassment escalates when there is lack of leadership among supervisors and administrators. For example, the military women were "not getting support from supervisors or administrators," according to the defence review. Confounding the issue is the fact that supervisors are often perpetrators, underlining the need for clear policies to protect employees from harassment as well as from retribution when they report harassment.

In 1996, Theresa Vince, a Sears training administrator in Ontario, was shot and killed by her supervisor, Russell Davis. Vince, 54, was slated to take early retirement mere days after the shooting. Davis' fixation on his senior staffer was well known and the source of office jokes.

"He'd call her in [to his office] it seemed about every 20 minutes," one employee testified at her inquest, "for basically trivial stuff." Although Vince had complained to head office more than a year previously, nothing was done.

"Sexual harassment in the workplace is only there because the people at the top condone it and maybe practice it themselves," according to Jim Vince, Theresa Vince's widowed husband.

Although harassment is often persistent, a single event may constitute sexual harassment. In 1999, Brigadier-General Larry Smith was about to be promoted to deputy Inspector-General, a job that included investigating sexual harassment in the U.S. military. That prompted General Claudia Kennedy, a three-star general, to testify that she had been sexually harassed by Smith. His promotion was cancelled.

Criminal assaults are a clear form of harassment, but the more subtle clashes between the values of many men and women in the workplace are also a factor. "Women have quite different styles than men and some men do not value the difference," Suek says. "They prefer the women who have a style similar to theirs and therefore similar to the dominant male culture."

Organizations have personalities, just like people, says Suek. "In some, the management style, the policies, the overall corporate culture reinforces respect, dignity and caring. Much of that starts at the top with the senior executives and is reinforced by the management and unions.

"Others allow people to bully and don't stop it. Gossip is mean and hurtful. Minorities are not valued and those attitudes are supported by senior management or the union," says Suek.

Complicating these differences are sexist attitudes used by many men to justify their offensive behaviour. "There are myths that women like the attention, when most women don't," says Gould. "As long as we maintain these myths, we will have harassment."

Addressing the Problem

Sexual harassment is a form of discrimination, even so called 'milder' forms. Writes Feary, "Pornography, sexual conversation, sexual and sexist jokes, girlie posters, and the like, are morally objectionable because they violate women's rights to enjoy fair equality of opportunity."

Investigating harassment is one of the specialities of Suek's firm, TLS Enterprises. After a complaint has been laid, Suek and her partners interview the parties involved, including the accused, the complainant and witnesses. Once the investigation is complete, they write a report explaining their conclusions and recommendations. It is up to the organization whether there will be any disciplinary actions or policy changes.

"The standard of proof is a 'balance of probabilities,'" Suck explains, "not 'beyond a reasonable doubt' as in criminal court. So we look to whether the circumstances are such that it 'probably' happened."

It may sound straightforward, but it rarely is. For example, there is often more than one complainant and more than one respondent. In such cases, an investigation reveals systemic sexual harassment is present, pointing to the need for further investigation or a larger organizational review.

Resolving specific complaints marks only the beginning—or the middle—of addressing the problem. "People who haven't been affected by harassment tend to think the issue is over once an investigation has taken place," explains Suek. "In fact, it is often a signal that the corporate culture has to be examined to determine how [harassment] can be prevented in the future."

Simply adopting a sexual harassment policy can give organizations a false sense of security. "Most often, they develop a policy and then forget about it until a crisis occurs," Suek observes.

Or they may say there isn't a problem because they haven't had a complaint. She describes how women in one organization who complained of harassment received dead rats in their mailboxes—for 'ratting-out' their fellow employees.

Changing Corporate Culture

Working to change the culture of the organization is the only way to prevent harassment, experts agree. And that means developing policies on respectful workplaces and implementing mechanisms for dealing with complaints. When complaints have been resolved, management must communicate to the rest of the staff that the situation has been remedied. Training to deal with all kinds of conflict, including bullying, harassment or disrespect are also part of the solution. At the

City of Winnipeg, 4,000 employees have completed the city's training on respectful workplace practices, boasts Gould, who handles harassment complaints as part of her job as the City of Winnipeg's employee relations consultant.

Many large corporations have taken a firm stand against sexual harassment. Dow Chemical fired 50 employees and disciplined 200 others in June 2001 for circulating pornographic images on company computers. In 2001, Xerox fired 40 workers for spending work time surfing pornographic sites, and *The New York Times* fired 22 employees for circulating offensive e-mails. Also in 2001, the Equal Employment Opportunity Commission in the U.S. filed the largest sexual harassment suit in its history against Mitsubishi, alleging harassment of 500 female employees.

Until problems surface, however, sexual harassment tends to be seen by managers as a 'soft issue,' not as important as something like finance. What they should remember, says Gould, "is that of the 100 most successful companies in Canada, the thing that sets apart the ones at the top is the time and effort spent on human capital." Treat employees well, respect them and your profit goes up.

"It sounds very simplistic, but the more that senior management models appropriate behaviour, the greater the likelihood that behaviour will be integrated into the workplace."

In smaller businesses, this may be difficult. Gould believes that the most vulnerable employees are those in small private companies. No union. No policies. No procedures. "It's often just them and the harasser," says Gould.

Unions are playing an increasingly important role in harassment protection. For example, the Canadian Union of Public Employees (CUPE) is developing contract language that includes all of the grounds covered by human rights legislation, including discrimination on the basis of sex and sexual orientation.

It wasn't always so. In the past, unions saw their duty of fair representation as a responsibility to defend only the person accused of harassment, says Maureen Morrison, a CUPE Equality Representative.

"Protecting the harasser under the guise of union solidarity allowed the boys to try to cover things up," she says. The increased participation of women in unions helped changed this practice, prompted by court cases that established that employers are responsible for maintaining a harassment-free workplace.

While union members accused of harassment are still represented by the unions, in keeping with the union's legal obligation, so are union members who make a harassment complaint. "This can be divisive," admits Morrison, "but it's part of a process of growth."

Today, union representatives like Morrison take the tack that "unions shouldn't try to protect people from their disrespectful behaviour."

At CUPE, negotiating policies on sexual harassment is part of a broader effort to support women-friendly policies including childcare, better family leave, better parental and maternity leave and pay equity.

When workplace grievance procedures are inadequate or nonexistent, sexual harassment complaints are made with human rights commissions (provincial or federal). A 17-year study of cases before the Canadian Human Rights Commission found that 75 percent of women who had filed complaints were no longer in their jobs. The study found that complainants often give up because the commission process can be time-consuming and often takes an emotional toll.

Another study found that the average sexual harassment complaint took more than two years to resolve. This points to another problem, namely that human rights commissions across the country tend to be hamstrung by a serious lack of funds.

"The people know what they are doing," Suek observes, "There just aren't enough of them or enough money."

Taking a Pro-Active Approach

Despite limited resources, the Manitoba Human Rights Commission 2000 annual report notes that the commission reduced the average time required to deal with complaints to 8.2 months. Nonetheless, harassment experts agree that the best way to stop harassment is to develop pro-active policies, rendering formal complaints a fail-safe measure of last resort.

Dealing with objectionable behaviour informally, through mediation or other workplace procedures, brings speedier results and can alleviate some of the stress on victims. A new federal government harassment policy extends beyond the legislated grounds of harassment of sex, race and sexual orientation to include personal harassment and abuse of authority. The policy encourages managers and employees to deal with conflicts at the outset.

Behaviour is one thing. Attitudes are another. That's why Gould stresses that "the remedy for harassment has to be substantive enough to have a positive change on the workplace culture."

The bottom line is that it is organizations' responsibility to ensure that managers "treat people with respect," says Gould. "You can't get any better than that."

WOMEN IN THE MILITARY

Elizabeth G. Book

Women now comprise nearly 15 percent of the U.S. military, Elizabeth G. Book reports in the following selection. Nevertheless, she reveals, women's participation in the armed forces continues to be controversial. For example, Book writes, many military women support the implementation of gender-integrated training; they argue that if men and women are going to work together, they should train together. However, others in the service criticize co-ed training as overly expensive, counterproductive, and demoralizing, Book explains. Furthermore, she points out, advisory commissions that have studied the issue have found that gender-separated training is more effective. Other controversial issues include women's serving in combat positions and the suitability of women sailors to serve aboard ships and submarines for long tours of duty. Book writes for *National Defense*, a magazine that reports on military issues.

Females comprised 14.7 percent of the armed forces in 2001, compared to 14.1 percent in 1998. That translates into approximately 200,000 women who serve as part of a 1.4-million active-duty force.

But despite the growing presence of women in the military services, controversies linger in some areas, particularly on the subjects of co-ed basic training and the suitability of female sailors to serve onboard ships.

A Pentagon advisory group known as DACOWITS (Defense Advisory Committee on Women in the Services) in recent years has advised the Defense Department on these issues.

Established in 1951, the DACOWITS has 30 to 40 members who counsel the secretary of defense on issues relating to women in the services. A Pentagon spokesman stated that members of DACOWITS devote personal time and resources to meet with service men and women around the world and "hear their concerns about matters related to their work, their living environment, their opportunities for advancement and their quality of life."

Training Men and Women Together

Female officers and officer candidates interviewed for this story generally agreed that, while controversial, gender-integrated training can help build camaraderie among recruits.

U.S. Naval Academy senior and midshipman first-class NaTasha McEachin said co-ed training should continue, because men and women are generally tasked with the same jobs and must work together. Ninety percent of jobs in the Navy are open to women, she noted. "It's a fact that men are more capable physically, but that does not mean that women can't do the job. If you're going to be working with people of the opposite sex, you're going to need to train with them."

"I don't have a problem with male-female training," said Cadet First Class Bethany Stott, a senior at the Air Force Academy. "You're going to have to work with them, so you should be trained together," she said. Stott said she believes that the mostly co-ed training that female Air Force Academy cadets go through make them more valuable to the military. "Women at the Air Force Academy are just as eager as men to serve and die for their country, if need be. There are certain career fields where you might not want someone who couldn't meet a certain physical standard, but if they can pass the physical test, that's cool."

Female Air Force cadets, said Stott, have gone through extensive training just to get where they are. "You wouldn't be here if you weren't willing to do that stuff," she said. "You have to be someone special to be part of an academy or join the military."

About 18 percent of the U.S. Air Force members are female.

Army Lt. Col. Anita Dixon, now serving as a congressional fellow to Rep. J.C. Watts, Jr., R-Okla., shared some of her experiences during two tours of duty as a peacekeeper in Bosnia. Dixon said that, because the military is now assigned more often to peace operations than combat operations, this "makes the need for women as peacekeepers quite evident." Women make up about 14.8 percent of the active-duty force.

"Women have a combination of qualities—a blend of soldier and social worker [that is] essential to the job as peacekeeper," Dixon said. "Women play a crucial role in a variety of jobs, and represent change in the way we serve our nation."

Objections to Gender Integration

However, not all service members favor efforts to standardize the roles of men and women in uniform. Brig. Gen. Ann Dunwoody, commanding officer of the Army's only airborne support command, told North Carolina's *Fayetteville Observer* that "Women are already forward deployed and engaged in today's nonlinear battlefield. We have to be cautious about policy initiatives that jeopardize our war-fighting direct-ground combat capability for the sake of social experimentation," she said.

"We serve in an integrated military, where diversity is considered a strength," Dunwoody said. "We no longer segregate by race, gender or religion. We're all one—we are all soldiers."

In 2000, then–Texas Governor George W. Bush was asked about his views on gender-integrated basic training. He referred to the work that his national security advisor Condoleezza Rice did as a member of the 1998 Federal Advisory Commission on Gender-Integrated Training and Related Issues, known as the Kassebaum-Baker Commission. Bush was quoted as saying, "I think women in the military have an important and good role, but the people who study the issue tell me that the most effective training would be to have the genders separated," he said.

Among the most outspoken critics of mixed-gender basic training is Elaine Donnelly, president of the Michigan-based Center for Military Readiness. "Secretary of Defense Donald H. Rumsfeld has said that he wants a faster, more deployable force. Co-ed training is out of sync with that philosophy, as it is more expensive, less efficient, creates problems that don't need to exist and has introduced sexual issues that don't need to be there," she said in an interview.

Donnelly has initiated a campaign with 15 other advocacy groups to end co-ed basic training in the Army, Navy and Air Force. The Marine Corps has kept its basic training gender segregated and does not plan to change that practice.

The coalition led by Donnelly sent a letter to Rumsfeld, asking him to end co-ed basic training, citing disciplinary problems that have been created in recent years, "as a direct result of gender-integrated basic training in the military."

The alliance, which included the Veterans of Foreign Wars, the American Legion and the Center for Security Policy, charged that "there is ample evidence that training men and women together complicates and detracts from the training mission." In contrast, the Marine Corps, which conducts gender-separated basic training, has enjoyed "remarkable success," said the letter. The coalition credits the Marines' basic training policies with the fact that their recruiting and retention numbers have remained consistently high. The Army, Air Force and Navy, according to the coalition, "have had to resort to costly bonuses, remedial instruction and weeks of time-consuming 'sensitivity training' to counter the negative effects of co-ed basic training."

Donnelly charged that "DACOWITS sees co-ed training as an equal opportunity women's issue, despite the information to the contrary," she said. "Co-ed training, at this point of the transformation of the services, costs more, detracts from discipline, and creates a need for an extra week of sensitivity training during basic training. This is demoralizing."

In the U.S. Navy, women constitute 14.3 percent of the active-duty force. Out of 55,000 women, about 18,000 serve on sea-duty—on surface ships only, since they are not allowed aboard submarines.

Women have been stationed aboard combat ships since 1994, and the proportion of women in ships' crews continues to increase, according to officials at the Bureau of Naval Medicine. "One of the most important recent challenges at sea is the introduction of women," said Navy Cmdr. Tom Javery. A physician who currently serves aboard the USS *Tarawa* (LHA), Javery explained why he believed the presence of women at sea complicates the job of the health care provider. "When a man comes to sick call with belly pain, it is probably one of two things—flu or appendicitis. When a woman comes in, it can be one of 50 things," he said.

Navy Cmdr. Josephine Brumit, a member of the Nurse Corps who is based at the Bureau of Naval Medicine (BMED), in Washington, D.C., disagreed with Javery's views. "There are many causes of abdominal pain in both men and women and the workup would be similar for non-gender specific causes of abdominal pain," she said. Brumit admitted that female stomach pain must be taken seriously because "there are important female specific ailments to consider such as ectopic pregnancy, which can be fatal."

However, she said, "testicular torsion, which is unique to males, is another serious medical problem with potential adverse outcome if not treated expediently."

Pregnancy at Sea

"Active-duty women are expected to plan their pregnancies around sea duty to limit shipboard crew losses," said Brumit. However, according to Navy Personnel Command statistics, 9.6 percent of women stationed aboard ships are lost each year due to pregnancy, she said. Brumit related that women may stay in their posts at sea until the 20th week of pregnancy, as long as prenatal care is available "within a time frame of six hours." An unwanted pregnancy potentially could derail a sailor's chance for promotion, because sea duty is "career enhancing," she said. Many sailors leave the ship because of pregnancy, and "we can't do anything about it," even though contraception is provided, said Brumit. "The Navy provides contraception to both male and female personnel aboard ships, including emergency contraception, which is an FDA-approved method of using oral contraceptive pills with specific dosing," she said.

Another concern for women at sea, Brumit said, is the availability of child care. Women who go to sea seek high-quality child care services, especially if they serve aboard a ship for a long period of time. DACOWITS has also addressed child care. A 1994 article by the Navy Office of Information included a recommendation that the Department of Defense should take additional steps to encourage expansion of the pool of child care services available to military personnel and their families.

CHAPTER 3

WOMEN'S MEDICAL AND REPRODUCTIVE RIGHTS

Contemporary Issues
Companion

Disparities in Women's Health Care

Alyson Reed

Women have never been treated as equal to men in the U.S. health-care system, according to Alyson Reed, a policy analyst for the American College of Nurse-Midwives. Historically, she explains, the medical profession considered the male body to be the norm for human health, with women differentiated primarily by their reproductive organs. However, Reed reports, researchers are increasingly discovering the flaws in this assumption: Women's overall physiology, medical problems, and health needs are very different from those of men. In addition, economic and social issues that affect women disproportionately—such as domestic violence and lack of access to health insurance—have not been addressed sufficiently by health-care policymakers, Reed contends. She argues that effective reforms must establish health care as a basic civil right for all people in the United States.

Access to health care has never been treated as a basic human right in the United States and has been viewed as a civil right only to the extent that it is denied to individuals on the basis of their race, sex, or membership in a "protected" class as defined by law. However, it is the ability to pay that continues to be the chief determinant of whether individuals can access health care. Although hospitals may not legally turn away patients who need emergency treatment, any other type of health care service is usually preconditioned on the source of payment, be it public or private.

Any discussion of women's health disparities, and discrimination against women in the context of the U.S. health care system, therefore needs to address the economic status of women and the role that economics plays in their ability to access health care and the quality of the health care services they receive. According to a 1997 guide on women's health issues published by the Institute of Medicine (IOM), the lack of preventive services for those without health insurance coverage "creates a deadly class disparity." (The IOM was chartered in 1970 by the prestigious National Academy of Sciences to enlist distin-

WOMEN'S MEDICAL AND REPRODUCTIVE RIGHTS

guished members of the appropriate professions in the examination of policy matters pertaining to the health of the public.) But economic class is not the only cause of disparities or discrimination in the health care field. A number of minority groups have traditionally suffered from discrimination based on race/ethnicity, sexual orientation, disability, age, and/or immigrant status. Finally, there is the overarching issue of gender-based discrimination, which is prevalent throughout American society and affects every aspect of women's lives, including their health, both physical and mental. Clearly, economic status, membership in a minority group, and gender are all overlapping and interacting factors in determining both access to health care services and the content of health care research.

A Historical Pattern of Discrimination

To understand gender-based discrimination in the health care field, it is important to understand the history of the U.S. health care system and women's interaction with health care providers. According to the IOM guide, "the medical enterprise, both in scientific research and in clinical practice, has traditionally viewed female lives and bodies through a lens of masculine experience and assumptions." A common medical view has been that the "female reproductive organs occupy a special realm, distinct from the body at large, and one that just happens to define their owner's essential nature." Under this model, the male body and male behavior were viewed as normative, while the female body was viewed as "other," with particular emphasis on the reproductive tract as setting women apart from men.

Given the gender breakdown within the health care professions, this history is not surprising. Women have traditionally been care givers for their families, and this expertise is reflected by women's dominance of the nursing and midwifery professions. Meanwhile, the better paid and higher status medical profession, which has an unfortunate history of excluding and resisting women physicians, remains dominated by men to this day. For reasons based on economic competition and sexist attitudes, many male physicians denigrated the female-dominated care-giving professions and asserted their role as the "experts" on the provision of women's health care. Despite this so-called expertise, women patients were frequently ignored, mistreated, not taken seriously, or denied access to needed services. For example, early gynecologists had an unfortunate history of "treating" women for symptoms such as nymphomania, epilepsy, and nervous and psychological problems, such as hysteria, by removing the ovaries and/or amputating the clitoris. As recently as the 1970s, a popular gynecology text advised gynecologists that the greatest diagnostic aid to use when listening to women's health complaints is the ability to distinguish "fact from fancy," implying that women were not to be taken seriously.

The Modern Women's Health Movement

The approval of the contraceptive pill by the Food and Drug Administration (FDA) in 1960 and the so-called sexual revolution which followed were profound events in the lives of women, not just for health reasons but also for their social and economic well-being. Approval of this new, highly effective contraceptive meant that women could now control their reproductive functions to an extent previously unknown. In conjunction with larger social transformations, this helped to reduce maternal mortality and morbidity rates, enabled women to pursue educational and employment opportunities not widely available earlier, and spurred a revolution in women's attitudes about their own sexuality and those of their partners. As a result of these developments, and women's frustration with their mistreatment by the male dominated health care establishment, the modern women's health movement was born, coinciding with the larger women's liberation movement of the early 1970s. As one history of the era has written, "The women's health movement was informed by the belief that women had the right to full and accurate information concerning diagnosis, treatment, and treatment alternatives; that women should be full partners in making decisions about their health; and that they were capable of making reasonable decisions given adequate, accurate information." Women were concerned about being undertreated (for conditions traditionally associated with men, like heart disease) and about being over-treated (for conditions associated with the reproductive cycle, such as uterine cancer). The care received by pregnant women is a good case in point. On the one hand, less than a third of uninsured pregnant women get proper prenatal care, while well-insured pregnant women suffer from many unnecessary medical interventions, such as cesarean sections, episiotomies, labor inductions and continuous electronic fetal monitoring. According to Dr. Stephen Thacker of the Centers for Disease Control and Prevention (CDC), the high rate of cesarean sections in the U.S. "is a major public health problem impacting health care delivery. Reducing the rate of cesarean section by five percent would save $800 million that could be spent on prenatal care and preventive programs."

Disparities Persist

Despite the progress made by the women's health movement, the health status of men and women is still not equal. The IOM guide offers many examples of these disparities, both in terms of access to care, treatment, and the quality of services received. While women live longer than men, they are also sicker than men. Although a greater percentage of girls survive through infancy and childhood, girls are at least twice as vulnerable to childhood sexual abuse as are boys, which is linked to major depression later in life. In fact, mental health disorders affect men and women in strikingly disparate patterns: women suffer more from manic depression, schizophrenia and phobias, while men have more substance abuse problems and antisocial personality disorders. Men tend to "externalize" mental distress, while women tend to "internalize" it. When it comes to screening, detection and treatment, women are frequently short-changed. For example, battering is a major factor in illness and injury among women, but is often overlooked by medical professionals. Men with AIDS are four times more likely to receive the "therapy of choice" than women, even when controlling for other factors, and treatment programs for alcoholics are usually based on the model of the male alcoholic, even though women alcoholics have very different needs and responses to treatment. For example, women are more likely to need a mental health assessment, treatment for depression, and support services, such as child care.

Due to illness, adult women spend more days confined to bed, take more time off from work, go to the hospital more, and see doctors more often, causing one expert to comment that "women don't suffer from unique conditions, they just report more of the same conditions reported by men." But this commentary cannot account for the vast disparities reported in the IOM guide, which posits that the disparities found in the health status of men and women stem from three sources: "different biologies and physiologies; divergent life courses; and unequal social statuses." Males and females have bodies that differ in important respects. They still have remarkably dissimilar experiences in growing up, during maturity, and as they age. And, despite the rapid social change of the last generation, they still play different roles in society and face different pressures and expectations. "We do not know, and perhaps never will," concludes the IOM, "just how much one's physical and mental state depends on culture and experience and how much on physiological and anatomical traits."

Perhaps the most important factor influencing health status is economic. As a group, women are far less able than men to pay for all of the health care services they need, primarily because they are paid less than men. Although a greater percentage of women are covered by some form of health plan, women more often depend on public sources of coverage than do men. As noted in the IOM guide, "Women in the childbearing years face the highest risk of inadequate coverage, at a time in their lives when the need is most acute." For low-income women, the lack of child care, adequate transportation, a dearth of providers willing to accept public insurance, and shortages of providers in rural and inner-city areas compound the problem of access.

These disparities in health status between men and women are further reinforced by the disparities in the area of clinical research. A major concern of the women's health movement has been that women are excluded from clinical trials. This exclusion has been based on fears among researchers that women's menstrual cycles and their potential for becoming pregnant might skew the results and/or harm the mother/fetus. Consequently, many conditions that disproportionately affect women have been understudied. Many researchers are particularly concerned about how the growing dominance of managed care has diminished the amount of private sector research funds available, leaving the government as the principal funder of health research. Unfortunately, this may result in a reversal of the improvements that have been observed in the area of women's health research in the 1990s.

Disparities Among Women

In addition to the health disparities between men and women, there are marked disparities among different subgroups of women. To document some of these differences, the National Institutes of Health published a *Women of Color Health Data Book* in 1998 with an exhaustive compilation of statistics relating to life expectancy, causes of death, behavior and lifestyle issues, utilization of health care services, access to health insurance and services, and morbidity and mortality rates associated with acute and chronic mental and physical conditions among women. In every category studied, significant disparities exist. In addition to the category of race/ethnicity, other studies undertaken by public and private researchers reveal that there are significant disparities in health status among adolescent, adult and elderly women, among heterosexual women and lesbians, among disabled and nondisabled women, among legal residents and illegal aliens, and perhaps most significantly, among different economic classes. These disparities intersect and overlap in ways that make it difficult to isolate their causes and thus propose remedies. For example, black women are four times more likely to die from pregnancy-related complications than are caucasian women, one of the largest racial disparities among major public health indicators.

Current Issues and Controversies

Given the disparities between men and women, and among various subgroups of women, a good deal of public attention has been focused on eliminating some of these gaps. Women's health issues have gained the attention of politicians, the media, and the health care industry, as women have flexed their economic and political muscles and become more vocal about getting access to the quality of health care they deserve. At the federal level, passage of the Violence Against Women Act, the Mothers and Newborn Protection Act, and increased spending levels for a variety of women's health initiatives, reflect the increasing political power of women, as both legislators and as voters. At the State level, hundreds of new laws have sought to address the specific health needs of women, particularly in the context of managed care. For example, in the 1990s, States have enacted measures specifically addressing coverage of FDA-approved contraceptive drugs and devices, breast reconstruction, breast and ovarian cancer screening, osteoporosis, mastectomy, standards for post-partum discharge, infertility, and direct access to providers of obstetrical and gynecological services. Central to most of these State initiatives is a response to the needs of middle and upper class women who already have health insurance coverage. Few, if any, of these laws apply to Medicaid or other indigent populations, while the number of women without any health insurance continues to grow.

Another troubling disparity for women relates to the treatment of pregnant women. While everyone can agree that access to maternity services is a desirable public health goal, we single out pregnant women for expanded insurance coverage while failing to provide similar coverage for contraceptive services. Women's health is about more than just childbearing. "The study of women's health has often paid more attention to the health of a woman's children than to the mother herself and devoted more resources to improving their welfare than hers," notes the IOM study. The tendency to view the health status of the fetus and the health status of women as separate or even oppositional concerns is an unfortunate trend in women's health. For example, in recent years, pregnant women who have tested positive for drug use have been incarcerated for child endangerment rather than treated for substance abuse, and childbearing women have been encouraged to undergo all kinds of unnecessary procedures to insure the well-being of the fetus, including some instances in which women have been ordered by the courts to have their children delivered by cesarean section against their will. As the IOM guide observes, "Over the past several decades, the obstetrician's primary concern has shifted from the mother to the fetus and newborn child."

Meanwhile, women are more likely to be the victims of domestic violence during pregnancy than at any other time during their lives. While major progress has been made in addressing violence against women, the unique needs of battered women are sometimes forgotten by policy makers. For example, when Congress enacted welfare reform legislation in 1996, women's advocates feared that the work requirements and time limits on benefits imposed under the new law would have a disparate impact on battered women. As a result, the law was amended to allow states to waive certain requirements for victims of domestic violence in their state welfare plans, while establishing a screening process that still left some advocates leery about exposing women to further harm by the system and/or their abusers. And like victims of rape, battered women are frequently the victims of sexist attitudes and gender-based discrimination by the very institutions that are supposed to be helping them. For example, battered women lose custody of their children to batterers in 40 to 70 percent of all custody disputes, and some insurance companies have sought to deny coverage for battered women on the grounds that they constitute a high-risk population.

Women who are immigrants to the U.S. may be at the greatest risk of all. In addition to the welfare reform legislation enacted in 1996, Congress also passed a new law severely limiting access to publicly-funded health services by immigrant populations, including legal residents of the U.S. Taken together, these two laws constitute a huge denial of access to health care services for those most vulnerable to poor health outcomes. Although the welfare law did not alter the Medicaid entitlement, early reports from the states show that there has been a precipitous decline in the Medicaid rolls, without a corresponding increase in employees with health insurance coverage. For immigrant women, even those here legally, the new law has had a chilling effect, creating a complex system of rules and exceptions that is virtually impossible to navigate even for many experienced policy advocates in the health care field, let alone by those for whom English is a second language.

Finally, and perhaps most importantly, the population of women without any health care coverage continues to grow. Despite all the efforts of women's health advocates to increase access to care, to improve the quality of services, to expand the field of women's health research, and to move more women into positions of power within the health care industry, this central disparity—between the haves and the have nots—still persists, and gets worse every day, even though our economy is thriving.

Recommendations for Reform

How do we begin to address the fundamental issues of discrimination and disparities in the field of women's health? The IOM report concludes that we must eliminate the "women's health ghetto," wherein women access the health care system primarily to seek care for their reproductive systems: "The segmented nature of women's health services has interfered with our ability to envision health care across the life span for women." But even if we succeed in developing a more holistic view of women's health, we will not have addressed the more basic issue for women: access and quality: "Spurred by women's unique psychological needs and often complicated by their particular social and economic situation, the challenge of navigating the costly and uncoordinated care system will grow no easier until thorough-going reform puts adequate health care within the reach of all Americans of both genders." For those concerned with civil rights, it is time to demand that access to health care be established as a basic human right for all people living in the U.S., regardless of their ability to pay.

INSURANCE COVERAGE OF WOMEN'S CONTRACEPTIVES

Marcia D. Greenberger

The following selection is taken from the September 10, 2001, testimony of Marcia D. Greenberger before the U.S. Senate on the issue of providing insurance coverage for women's contraceptives. Greenberger explains that many health insurance companies provide little or no coverage of prescription contraceptive drugs and devices used exclusively by women, such as the IUD and the birth-control pill. Contraception is an essential part of basic health care for women, she argues, enabling them to avoid the high monetary and health costs of unintended pregnancy. The exclusion of prescription contraceptives from insurance plans that cover other prescription drugs is discriminatory, Greenberger maintains, because it places unfair economic burdens on women. She proposes that federal legislation should be passed that requires all health plans to provide coverage of prescription contraceptives. Greenberger is the co-president of the National Women's Law Center in Washington, D.C., which works to secure and defend women's legal rights.

Access to reliable contraception is essential to women's health, and the failure of insurers to cover it has far-reaching consequences for the health of women and the health of their children. The court in *Erickson v. Bartell Drug Co.*, got it exactly right in its June 2001 decision when it said, "the exclusion of prescription contraceptives creates a gaping hole in the coverage offered to female employees, leaving a fundamental and immediate healthcare need uncovered."

Pregnancy prevention is central to good health care for women. Most women have the biological potential for pregnancy for over 30 years of their lives, and for approximately three-quarters of her reproductive life, the average woman is trying to postpone or avoid pregnancy. Over half of pregnancies in the United States are unintended. Access to contraception is critical to preventing unwanted pregnancies (and thus also to reducing the number of abortions), and to

Excerpted from Marcia D. Greenberger's testimony before the Committee on Health, Education, Labor, and Pensions of the U.S. Senate, September 10, 2001.

enabling women to control the timing and spacing of their pregnancies, which in turn reduces the incidence of maternal morbidity, low
birth weight babies, and infant mortality.

A Lack of Coverage for Contraception

Despite the importance of contraception to women's health, private
health insurance has failed to provide adequate coverage of prescription contraceptive drugs and devices and related services. Almost half
of all fee-for-service large-group plans (those covering over 100
employees) do not cover any form of contraception at all, and only
one-third cover oral contraceptives, the most commonly used form of
reversible contraceptive in the United States. Although managed care
plans typically provide better coverage than traditional fee-for-service
plans, only 39% of HMOs routinely cover the five methods of
reversible contraception. Only 49% of large-group plans and 39% of
small-group plans cover outpatient annual exams—which are essential for women using prescription contraceptive drugs or devices.
Before Congress mandated contraceptive coverage for federal employees, 81% of the plans in the Federal Employees Health Benefits Program (FEHBP) did not cover all five reversible methods of contraception, and 10% of the plans did not cover any of these methods. The
failure of private insurance plans to cover contraceptives is even more
glaring when one considers that 97% of traditional fee-for-service
plans cover other prescription drugs.

Women who do not have health insurance coverage for contraception, but who nonetheless wish to avoid pregnancy, are often forced
to use a less expensive, but also less effective, method of contraception. A woman without insurance coverage also may not be able to
afford to use the contraceptive method that is most appropriate for
her medical and personal circumstances. For example, an IUD or
implant may be the most appropriate form of contraception for some
women (for example, where oral contraceptives are contraindicated
for medical reasons), but these devices have the highest initial cost
and therefore can be the hardest to pay for out-of-pocket.

Moreover, some insurance plans do not cover oral contraceptives
even when they are prescribed for health reasons other than birth
control—for example, for medical conditions like dysmenorrhea and
pre-menstrual syndrome, or to help prevent ovarian cancer. Thus, in
addition to the dangers to women's health presented by the failure of
insurance to cover pregnancy prevention, the exclusion of contraception from insurance coverage causes other harmful consequences for
women's health.

Contraceptive Coverage Is a Matter of Equity

Not only is pregnancy a condition that is unique to women, but the
only forms of prescription contraception available today are exclu-

sively for women (oral contraceptives, injections like Depo Provera and Lunelle, implants like Norplant, IUDs, and barrier methods like the diaphragm and cervical cap). Thus, the exclusion of prescription contraceptives from health insurance coverage unfairly disadvantages women by singling out for unfavorable treatment a health insurance need that only women have. Failure to cover contraception forces women to bear higher health care costs to avoid pregnancy, and exposes women to the unique physical, economic and emotional consequences that can result from unintended pregnancy.

The most immediate economic consequence for women is the out-of-pocket cost of paying for contraception. American women spend about 68 percent more than men in out-of-pocket health care costs, and much of this disparity can be attributed to the lack of adequate coverage of reproductive health services. Such costs make up one-third of all health care costs for women under private health insurance policies. Moreover, when effective contraception is not used, it is women who bear the risk of unwanted pregnancy. When unintended pregnancy results, it is women who incur the attendant physical burdens and medical risks of pregnancy, women who disproportionately bear the health care costs of pregnancy and childbirth, and women who often face barriers to employment and educational opportunities as a result of pregnancy, even today despite the fact that the law clearly prohibits this form of discrimination in the workplace and in educational institutions.

In short, forcing women to pay out of pocket to cover their contraceptive needs is both harmful to their health and manifestly unfair. It is no wonder that when many insurance plans agreed to covered Viagra as soon as it received FDA approval—while continuing to exclude prescription contraception—an outcry ensued.

Employers Must Provide Contraceptive Coverage

Women's ability to receive the contraceptive insurance coverage they need has advanced significantly with two recent interpretations of the federal civil rights laws, one by the Equal Employment Opportunity Commission (EEOC) and one by a federal court. Both held that it is unlawful sex discrimination in the workplace under Title VII of the Civil Rights Act of 1964, and specifically the Pregnancy Discrimination Act of 1978 (PDA) that is incorporated in Title VII, for an employer covered by Title VII to exclude prescription contraceptive drugs and devices and related services from a health insurance plan provided to its employees, when the plan covers other prescription drugs and devices and preventive care generally.

Title VII prohibits all private employers with at least 15 employees, and public employers as well, from discriminating on the basis of sex in the terms and conditions of employment, including in fringe benefits. And Congress made explicit, when enacting the PDA as an amendment to Title VII, that pregnancy-related discrimination constitutes illegal discrimination on the basis of sex in all terms and conditions of employment, including employer-provided insurance. This legislation explicitly overruled the Supreme Court's 1976 decision in *General Electric Co. v. Gilbert*, which had held that an otherwise comprehensive short-term disability policy that excluded pregnancy-related disabilities from coverage did not discriminate on the basis of sex in violation of Title VII.

Based on Title VII, and specifically the PDA, both the EEOC and the *Erickson* federal court have underscored that an employer who singles out pregnancy-related health care—including contraception—for disadvantageous treatment in an employee health benefits plan is committing unlawful sex discrimination. In December 2000, the EEOC issued a formal statement of Commission policy holding that Title VII prohibits employers from excluding prescription contraceptive coverage from an employee health plan that otherwise covers prescription drugs and devices generally as well as a wide range of other preventive health care. The Commission reasoned that Title VII's "prohibition on discrimination against women based on their ability to become pregnant . . . necessarily includes a prohibition on discrimination related to a woman's use of contraceptives." According to the EEOC, this means that employers must cover the expenses of prescription contraceptives and related medical services to the same extent and on the same terms that they cover the expenses of other drugs, devices and preventative services. As the federal agency charged with administering and enforcing Title VII, the EEOC's interpretation of the law is authoritative and entitled to substantial deference. And both Attorney General John Ashcroft and EEOC Chair Cari Dominguez have stated that they will uphold this ruling.

The Court Upholds Contraceptive Coverage

The EEOC's ruling was followed by the decision in *Erickson v. Bartell Drug Co.* in June of 2001, in which the U.S. District Court for the Western District of Washington found that the defendant's exclusion of prescription contraceptives from its otherwise comprehensive employee health benefits plan constitutes a violation of Title VII. The court's decision, granting summary judgment to Jennifer Erickson and the plaintiff class she represents, was the first one ever to rule definitively on the merits of this issue—although two other courts have also recently ruled in favor of the plaintiffs in similar cases, denying the defendants' motions to dismiss and allowing the cases to proceed. In the *Erickson* decision, the court carefully reviewed the legislative history of Title VII and the PDA, relevant precedents, the EEOC Decision, and each of the arguments presented by the defendant. The court concluded:

Bartell's exclusion of prescription contraception from its prescription plan is inconsistent with the requirements of federal law. The PDA is not a begrudging recognition of a limited grant of rights to a strictly defined group of women who happen to be pregnant. Read in the context of Title VII as a whole, it is a broad acknowledgment of the intent of Congress to outlaw any and all discrimination against any and all women in the terms and conditions of their employment, including the benefits an employer provides to its employees. Male and female employees have different, sex-based disability and healthcare needs, and the law is no longer blind to the fact that only women can get pregnant, bear children, or use prescription contraception.

On this basis, the court ordered Bartell Drug Co., the defendant, to cover each of the available options for prescription contraception to the same extent, and on the same terms, that it covers other drugs, devices, and preventive care for its employees, as well as all contraception-related outpatient services. Bartell has subsequently notified its employees that these drugs, devices, and services are now covered.

As a result of the EEOC and court rulings, all employers covered by Title VII are now on notice of their legal obligation to include coverage of prescription contraceptives if they are providing health insurance to their employees that otherwise covers proscription drugs and devices and preventive care. We are pleased that some have responded on their own by promptly adding this coverage to their employee health plans. Other employers have added contraceptive coverage after being pressed to do so by their employees. For example, in April 2001, after several female faculty and staff members at the University of Nebraska urged the university administration to add contraceptive coverage—with legal assistance from the National Women's Law Center—the university Regents agreed. . . .

Extending Coverage to All Women

Although the Title VII rulings represent significant progress for the employer-provided plans covered by Title VII, enactment of the Equity in Prescription Insurance and Contraceptive Coverage Act (EPICC) is critical to ensuring that all health plans that provide coverage of prescription drugs include the same level of coverage for FDA-approved prescription contraceptives, as well as coverage for outpatient contraceptive services. EPICC does not require special treatment of contraceptives—only equitable treatment within the context of an existing prescription drug benefit. Because the vast majority of insurance plans cover prescription drugs, a large majority of insured women are expected to benefit from the expanded access to contraceptive coverage that EPICC will produce.

EPICC will extend protection beyond that provided by Title VII. It will cover plans not provided by an employer to its employees, such as non-employment group and individual plans, and those employer plans not covered by Title VII. Millions of women receive their insurance from a source not covered by Title VII. An estimated 16 million Americans obtain health insurance from private insurance other than employer-provided plans. This includes people who are self-employed; those employed by employers who offer no health insurance; part-time, temporary, and contract workers; early retirees too young for Medicare; and unemployed or disabled people not eligible for public insurance. Women are disproportionately represented in several of these categories, such as part-time, temporary, and contract workers. Moreover, not everyone who receives health insurance through an employer is protected by Title VII, which applies only to employers with 15 or more employees—this is less than a fifth of all U.S. employers, and some 14 million workers are employed by entities that fall beneath this threshold.

We know from the unfortunate experience with maternity coverage after passage of the PDA that it is critical to guarantee coverage for women who do not receive their health insurance through their employers. Before the PDA's enactment, private health insurance often did not include maternity care—basic prenatal and delivery services—in their standard policies. Following passage of the PDA, which made clear that employers covered by Title VII could not single out for exclusion from an employee health plan the medical expenses related to pregnancy and childbirth, insurers began to include maternity benefits in their standard benefit package for employer-sponsored plans because their customers, the employers, were legally obligated to provide that benefit. But, because there is no legal mandate to do so, insurers do not always include maternity benefits in their standard benefits package for individuals or others not covered through an employer. There is every reason to believe that insurers will respond in a similar way to contraceptive coverage, thereby underscoring the importance of EPICC.

State experience reinforces the wisdom of EPICC's approach. Sixteen states have passed new laws requiring health plans that cover prescription drugs to cover prescription contraceptives. Their passage confirms the growing recognition of the importance of this issue, and the appropriateness of this approach. But women's access to this basic benefit should not depend on where they live.

Contraceptive Coverage Is Cost-Effective

As is true for other key forms of preventive health care, coverage of contraceptives can actually save money. For every dollar spent to provide publicly funded contraceptive services, an average of $3.00 is saved just in Medicaid costs for pregnancy-related health care and medical care for newborns. And, studies by business groups and employer consultants have concluded that employers can save money by including contraceptive coverage in their employee health plans, thereby reducing unintended pregnancies and their associated costs, as well as promoting maternal and child health. For example, the Washington Business Group on Health, an organization that represents 160 national and multinational employers, has estimated that failing to provide contraceptive coverage could cost an employer at least 15% more than providing this coverage. Their report concluded, "For health and financial reasons, employers concerned with providing both comprehensive and cost-effective health benefits ought to consider ensuring that they are covering the full range of contraceptive options."

Moreover, any direct premium costs to an employer who adds contraceptive coverage to its benefits plan are at most extremely modest, and likely to be nonexistent. The concrete experience of the Federal Employees Health Benefits Program (FEHBP) is most instructive. It showed that adding contraceptive coverage to the FEHBP caused no increase in the federal government's premium costs. When the FEHBP contraceptive coverage requirement was implemented, the Office of Personnel Management (OPM), which administers the program, arranged with the health carriers to adjust the 1999 premiums in 2000 to reflect any increased insurance costs due to the addition of contraceptive coverage. However, no such adjustment was necessary, and OPM reported that "there was no cost increase due to contraceptive coverage." Another study found that on average, it costs a private employer only an additional $1.43 per month per employee to add coverage for the full range of FDA-approved reversible contraceptives.

Of course, even if the cost of contraceptive coverage were substantial—which, as shown, it most assuredly is not—such costs could not justify shortchanging women or sacrificing their health. It would be unthinkable to exclude insurance coverage for heart disease or many other conditions that can lead to expensive health care because of cost. Cost is never recognized as a defense to discrimination, as both the EEOC and the court in *Erickson* noted, and it should not be used as a reason—let alone an unsupported assertion, as would be the case here—to penalize women.

The Public Supports Contraceptive Coverage

Not surprisingly, there is broad public support for laws requiring contraceptive coverage. One recent poll conducted in June 2001 found that 77% of Americans support laws requiring health insurance plans to cover prescription contraception. This support has been steady. A 1998 Kaiser Family Foundation poll found that 75% of Americans believe contraception should be covered by insurers even if such coverage added to the cost. This broad public support is also reflected in the growing number of states that have enacted legislation requiring all health insurance plans to cover prescription contraceptives, and the fact that in many additional states such legislation is now pending. And, of course, the federal government has also recognized the importance of this benefit by providing it to federal employees.

Unless Congress acts, women will not have the contraceptive insurance coverage that they need and deserve. EPICC would provide that coverage, and represents a major step forward for women's health.

NEW OPTIONS FOR PREVENTING AND ENDING PREGNANCY

Ellen Chesler

In recent years, women have gained more options to choose from in preventing conception or terminating a pregnancy, writes Ellen Chesler. For example, she reports, emergency contraception (often called the morning-after pill) is designed to prevent pregnancy up to seventy-two hours after unprotected intercourse. Due to technological advances, surgical abortion has become safer and simpler and can be performed at much earlier stages of pregnancy than was the case when abortion was first legalized in 1973. In addition, women now have access to the drug mifepristone (RU-486), which can be used terminate a pregnancy without surgery up to the seventh week. However, Chesler points out, abortion foes object to these new procedures, and the ensuing political controversy has made it difficult for women to access all their reproductive options. Chesler is the director of the Program on Reproductive Health and Rights at the Open Society Institute and the author of *Woman of Valor: Margaret Sanger and the Birth Control Movement in America*.

In recent years, medical science has devised new options for very early termination of unwanted pregnancy, measures that did not exist when *Roe v. Wade* was decided in 1973. In addition to widening the range of choices for women, these advances—most notably the "morning-after" contraceptive and the abortion pill mifepristone (RU-486)—are likely to alter the imagery and the politics of abortion dramatically. Where the so-called pro-life movement has capitalized on a tiny number of late procedures involving fetuses with the features of babies, the new technology makes plain that most abortions involve microscopic embryos. This shifts the moral as well as the medical terrain for most people, as the country's debate over embryonic-stem-cell research makes clear. Unless the radical right succeeds in overturning *Roe v. Wade*, these new scientific developments bode well for the pro-choice movement in this country.

Nevertheless, the abortion debate often seems, as Robin Toner put it in *The New York Times,* frozen in time. This is true despite the fact that how, when, and where an unwanted pregnancy is terminated today involves medical, moral, and practical considerations that didn't exist when *Roe v. Wade* was decided more than a quarter of a century ago. Indeed, nearly everything about abortion has changed since then except for the way we think and talk about it. With public-opinion polls showing that a clear majority of Americans support comprehensive sex education, family planning, and the individual right to terminate a pregnancy safely, these new scientific and medical developments need to enter public discourse and shape it.

Emergency Contraception

First, there is the matter of "emergency contraception," more commonly known as the morning-after pill, which works up to 72 hours after unprotected sex by preventing fertilization or by interrupting the implantation of a fertilized ovum in the uterine wall so that a pregnancy never occurs. The regimen is well known and widely used in western Europe, where a dedicated product is now available without prescription. The French distribute it in high schools.

For years, physicians in the United States have routinely broken up packages of standard birth-control pills and administered consecutive double doses of them to women who report unprotected intercourse and fear unwanted conception. The procedure, which produces moderate nausea but no other side effects, is prevalent on many college campuses. Yet pill manufacturers here—perhaps fearing protests by anti-*abortion* zealots or cannibalization of the market for standard oral contraceptives—year after year declined to market a dedicated product, and the Food and Drug Administration only recently approved one, after nearly a decade of effort by reproductive-rights groups.

The FDA is now considering a petition to bring emergency contraception over the counter, but for the time being it needs to be made widely available through primary-care doctors working with local pharmacists. Estimates suggest that emergency contraception alone could prevent half of all unintended pregnancies—still about three million a year in the United States, half of which result in surgical abortion.

The emergency-contraception method is especially warranted as a backup to condoms, which as a result of successful education and social marketing are now widely used in this country to protect against sexually transmitted disease. Condoms also work as barrier contraceptives, of course, and according to the Alan Guttmacher Institute, better use of contraception accounts for about three-quarters of the 21 percent decline in adolescent pregnancy rates between 1990 and 1997. The problem is that condoms have a high failure rate and require a backup—or a "Plan B," as the marketers are calling their new dedicated product.

Early Termination of Pregnancy

As Americans come to understand and access the new "morning-after" opportunities, they also need to be made aware of the new "month-after" options, since it is after missing their menstrual period that most women first suspect that they are pregnant. Relatively few Americans, including public officials, realize that when *Roe* first became the law of the land, a woman could not even confirm a pregnancy until she was seven weeks or more into gestation. To terminate it, she had to wait a least several more weeks, until her cervix softened, so that a doctor could insert the metal surgical instrument then necessary to perform a standard dilation and curettage of the uterus.

Today, by contrast, an inexpensive urine test that can confirm pregnancy in its earliest stages by registering hormonal changes is available for home use. The recent approval of mifepristone (long known as RU-486) means that the pregnancy, if unwanted, can be ended as soon as it is detected. Regulations in the United States permit use of this oral medication up to the seventh week of pregnancy—though in some parts of Europe and Asia, hundreds of thousands of women are using it effectively up to the ninth week without adverse consequences. The simple regimen actually requires a combination of two pills taken in sequence: mifepristone, which blocks the production of hormones needed to sustain pregnancy, followed by misoprostol, which induces moderate uterine contractions and produces the equivalent of a heavy menstrual period that lasts up to five days.

The crucial distinction between mifepristone and emergency contraceptives is that the former eliminates a fertilized ovum whereas the latter prevents the ovum from being fertilized. In other respects, mifepristone's effects do not differ much from what many women experience every month from menarche (their first menstrual period) to menopause (their last)—when they eliminate unfertilized eggs along with the contents of the uterine lining, without much fuss over the loss. The bleeding is heavier—the cramps more intense—but the process is not substantially different. Indeed, research confirms that about half of all conceptions spontaneously abort very early—generally before the woman even realizes she was pregnant—and pass away naturally, experienced as late and heavy menstruation.

A Comprehensive Approach

One can see the promise of these new approaches in a small and friendly community-based family health center that operates out of a storefront near downtown Brooklyn, New York. Here, at the New Options Training Center, as it is being called, a revolution is brewing in how family planning and early-abortion care are provided. Pioneered by a team of committed young physicians and nurse practitioners, the facility is among the first family-medicine centers in the United States to integrate reproductive health care, including early-abortion services, into general medicine. This allows each patient to experience a continuum of care—from family-planning visits to morning-after prescriptions or early abortion, if needed—as part of her ordinary medical visit. Gone is the stigma that has been associated with the termination of unwanted pregnancy since abortion was legalized more than a quarter of a century ago, and for the many years before, when it was clandestine and illegal yet widely available.

Affiliated with the Long Island College Hospital, one of Brooklyn's most venerable institutions, the family health center sits less than a mile from the makeshift clinic in a Brownsville tenement where Margaret Sanger made history in 1916 by defying the law to provide contraceptives to women, many of whom were immigrants. Sanger went to jail for 30 days, but subsequent appeal of her conviction established a medical exception to the New York State laws prohibiting birth control and granted doctors (though not nurses, as Sanger had hoped) the right to prescribe contraceptives for health reasons only.

The birth-control movement in America nonetheless remained a target of legal repression and political controversy. It developed under these difficult circumstances only through the slow but steady growth of independent, not-for-profit clinics affiliated with the Planned Parenthood movement, in isolation from mainstream medicine. Lost was Sanger's vision of a comprehensive program of preventive public health, with clinics in every urban neighborhood and traveling caravans of medical personnel in rural areas providing a full range of services. Only after 50 years of sustained advocacy and litigation—following *Griswold v. Connecticut*, the historic 1965 decision in which the U.S. Supreme Court struck down state laws banning birth control used by married couples—did President Lyndon Johnson finally incorporate family planning into America's still fledgling public-health and social-welfare programs.

When abortion was legalized in 1973, however, the earlier pattern was replicated. Federal funding was denied, and today only 15 states provide Medicaid coverage of abortion. Abortion services quickly moved out of hospitals into freestanding clinics that in some cases are administered by Planned Parenthood but mostly run privately and for profit. In the increasingly hostile climate that has since surrounded the practice in this country, providers have become true heroes, braving harassment and violence, and even risking death. Not surprisingly, their numbers have decreased dramatically, down 14 percent in recent years to a mere few thousand nationwide. Ninety-five percent of the country's rural counties today have no abortion services and, statistically, seven states have fewer than one provider per 100,000 women.

With the graying of a generation of doctors motivated by memories of the horrors of illegal abortion, the problem has become particularly acute. Abortion training is not routinely provided as part of medical residency training, even for obstetricians and gynecologists.

And while committed medical students around the country—more and more of them women—have begun to demand the reversal of this practice, wisdom may prevail in moving back to the future, so to speak, by reclaiming Margaret Sanger's vision of comprehensive neighborhood health centers.

Realizing a Promise

If the radical right has its way, however, clinics such as these will be suppressed. The intense politics of abortion have already resulted in the dissemination of much misinformation about the abortion pill among providers and patients—not to mention politicians. The first challenge for innovative services like the New Options facility in Brooklyn is to overcome these distortions with education and training akin to what has worked in the past with new methods of contraception. A second challenge is to untangle the thicket of legal provisions and administrative codes that govern abortion at the state and local levels and make it a more intensely regulated procedure than, say, brain surgery.

New Options is providing family practitioners with a working model of comprehensive reproductive health care, including how early abortion can be integrated into their practices. This includes hands-on training in emergency contraception, medical abortion, and early-gestational ultrasound as well as information on the many administrative issues involved in implementing early abortion services—such as complex consent forms, proper medical-waste disposal, malpractice requirements, unusual billing protocols for third-party payers and Medicaid, and, sadly, enhanced security measures. Lawyers, meanwhile, are researching how to revise state laws to permit nurse practitioners to dispense the month-after pill with appropriate physician backup. Despite many obstacles, the pilot project in Brooklyn has attracted some 20 patients a week since it opened early in 2001, and it is now ready to train medical residents from eight family-medicine programs that together produce 60 new doctors each year. Success has been so rapid that the Continuum Health Partners, of which Long Island College Hospital is a member, is ready to sponsor a second site.

Making New Techniques Available

Approximately half of those who terminate early pregnancies at New Options choose mifepristone. The others are opting for a simple mechanical procedure that evacuates the uterine contents without trauma and provides an alternative to the pill or a backup on the rare occasions when it fails. This process, manual vacuum aspiration of the uterus, uses an inexpensive handheld device called a cannula that creates a gentle suction strong enough to dislodge a tiny embryo. It replaces the earlier technology of a large and expensive electric suction machine and is a variation on menstrual-extraction techniques used long ago. But the new technology makes the procedure safer, cheaper, and more accessible than earlier methods—one that can be easily administered in comprehensive primary-health-care settings or in the doctors' offices. This too, however, requires training.

Pilot projects using such methods are now also under way in existing abortion clinics, in Planned Parenthood facilities where abortion has not been provided in the past, and in other primary settings. In New York, these include the maternity-and-infant-care centers run by organizations such as New York's Community Healthcare Network and Metropolitan Health and Research Association. Elsewhere in the country, progress is slower, with only a dozen or so residency-training programs having expressed willingness to undertake programs. The potential, however, is enormous, with 121 medical schools nationwide, supervising 253 residency programs in obstetrics gynecology, 487 in family medicine, and 393 in internal medicine. Providing midlevel service would also require training of nurses and skilled midwives, but to achieve meaningful scale much broader investment will be required.

When the FDA finally approved mifepristone late in 2000 in the waning days of the Clinton administration, an unrealistic euphoria set in about the transforming possibilities of the new drug. Few beyond the community of existing providers acknowledged the many obstacles that must be overcome before the new method can be integrated into mainstream reproductive care. Still, the potential is there, as early successes now demonstrate.

Surgical abortions in the United States already take place considerably earlier than in the past: More than half are performed within eight weeks of conception, and nearly 90 percent occur within 12 weeks. A growing body of evidence points to an increasing eagerness by patients and clinicians to push the process even earlier and to integrate it back into standard medical practice. The timing is right in view of growing national trends toward providing primary preventive care in neighborhood facilities affiliated with managed-care plans and hospitals, like the New Options center in Brooklyn.

The Politics of Abortion

George W. Bush notwithstanding, the political environment is also ripe for this development. Despite deliberate efforts by both major candidates in 2000's presidential election to duck the issue, abortion rights registered a surprising third place as a concern in at least two major exit polls—just behind the much belabored campaign subjects of Social Security and education, and ahead of taxes. Independent women abandoned the Bush candidacy in droves despite his effort to appear compassionate in his conservatism, and the gender gap turned into a chasm, with a record 22-point divide in how men and women voted.

Since his inauguration, the situation has further deteriorated for

Bush politically, with criticism of his policy restricting research on stem cells harvested from very early embryos having now become the defining issue of the first year of his presidency. As the country engages in an unprecedented national conversation about early microbiology and gestational development, it is only a matter of time before voters more fully comprehend the implications and meanings of the distinctions between stages of embryonic and fetal development. The result is likely to be increasing levels of support for early and safe abortion.

Margaret Sanger and George W. Bush span a turbulent century, but the gulf between them may not be as wide as it seems. Bush's maternal grandmother, after all, was a supporter of Planned Parenthood of Connecticut, and his father as a Republican member of Congress from Texas in the 1960s joined in bipartisan support for those first federal family-planning programs. This President Bush and his political advisers may never see the wisdom of affirmatively endorsing early options to end unwanted pregnancies and integrating them into the continuum of safe, affordable, and accessible reproductive health care for American women. But ironically, his presidency may engender the public schooling in basic biology that makes it happen.

LEGAL ABORTION IS NOT NECESSARY TO PROTECT WOMEN'S HEALTH

Clarke D. Forsythe

In the following selection, attorney Clarke D. Forsythe writes that although most Americans are morally opposed to abortion, they want it to remain legal because they believe that otherwise women's health will be put at risk. According to Forsythe, this attitude stems from four prevalent myths about abortion's effect on women's health, including the argument that making abortion illegal will result in thousands of deaths from "back-alley" abortions. In fact, he asserts, the number of women who died from abortions prior to legalization has been drastically exaggerated; furthermore, women still die each year from complications of legal abortions. He concludes that legal abortion has not improved women's health, emphasizing the adverse impact it has had on both women and their unborn children. Forsythe is the president of Americans United for Life, an organization that opposes abortion.

Twenty-six years after the Supreme Court's *Roe v. Wade* decision, the public debate on abortion seems to have reached a stalemate. The issue continues to be debated in Congress and state legislatures across the country, but, year to year, there seems to be little change in public opinion.

This does not mean, however, that the abortion issue is going to recede in intensity any time soon. There are many reasons for this, but perhaps the most important is simply that "the majority of Americans morally disapprove of the majority of abortions currently performed," as University of Virginia sociologist James Hunter concludes in his path-breaking 1994 book, *Before the Shooting Begins: Searching for Democracy in America's Culture Wars*. Hunter's analysis is based on the 1991 Gallup poll "Abortion and Moral Beliefs," the most thorough survey of American attitudes toward abortion yet conducted.

The Gallup study found that 77 percent of Americans believe that abortion is at least the "taking of human life" (28 percent), if not

Excerpted from "Abortion Is Not a 'Necessary Evil,'" by Clarke D. Forsythe, *Christianity Today*, May 24, 1999. Copyright © 1999 by Christianity Today, Inc. Reprinted with permission.

"murder" itself (49 percent). Other polls confirm these findings. And yet, while many Americans—perhaps 60 percent in the middle—see legalized abortion as an evil, they see it as "necessary."

The *Chicago Tribune* aptly summarized the situation in a September 1996 editorial: "Most Americans are uncomfortable with all-or-nothing policies on abortion. They generally shy away from proposals to ban it in virtually all circumstances, but neither are they inclined to make it available on demand no matter what the circumstances. They regard it, at best, as a necessary evil."

If Middle America—as Hunter calls the 60 percent—sees abortion as an evil, why is it thought to be necessary? Although the 1991 Gallup poll did not probe this question specifically, it made clear that it is not because Middle America sees abortion as necessary to secure equal opportunities for women. For example, less than 30 percent believe abortion is acceptable in the first three months of pregnancy if the pregnancy would require a teenager to drop out of school (and the number drops below 20 percent if the abortion is beyond three months). Likewise, less than 20 percent support abortion in the first three months of pregnancy if the pregnancy would interrupt a woman's career (and that support drops to 10 percent if the abortion is after the third month).

Four "Necessary" Myths

Instead, many Americans, therefore, may see abortion as "necessary" to avert "the back alley." In this sense, the notion of legal abortion as a "necessary evil" is based on a series of myths widely disseminated since the 1960s. These myths captured the public mind and have yet to be rebutted.

Myth #1: One to two million illegal abortions occurred annually before legalization. In fact, the annual total in the few years before abortion on demand was no more than tens of thousands and most likely fewer. For example, in California, the most populous state where it was alleged that 100,000 illegal abortions occurred annually in the 1960s, only 5,000 abortions were performed in 1968, the first full year of legalization.

Myth #2: Thousands of women died annually from abortions before legalization. As a leader in the legalization movement, Dr. Bernard Nathanson later wrote: "How many deaths were we talking about when abortion was illegal? In N.A.R.A.L. [the National Abortion Rights Action League] we generally emphasized the drama of the individual case, not the mass statistics, but when we spoke of the latter it was always '5,000 to 10,000 deaths a year.' I confess that I knew the figures were totally false, and I suppose that others did too if they stopped to think of it. But in the 'morality' of our revolution, it was a useful figure, widely accepted, so why go out of our way to correct it with honest statistics?"

In fact, the U.S. Centers for Disease Control (CDC) statistics in 1972 show that 39 women died from illegal abortion and 27 died from legal abortion.

Myth #3: Abortion law targeted women rather than abortionists before legalization. In fact, the nearly uniform policy of the states for nearly a century before 1973 was to treat the woman as the second victim of abortion.

Myth #4: Legalized abortion has been good for women. In fact, women still die from legal abortion, and the general impact on health has had many negative consequences, including the physical and psychological toll that many women bear, the epidemic of sexually transmitted disease, the general coarsening of male-female relationships over the past 30 years, the threefold increase in the repeat-abortion rate, and the increase in hospitalizations from ectopic pregnancies.

Refuting the Myths

A generation of Americans educated by these myths sees little alternative to legalized abortion. It is commonly believed that prohibitions on abortion would not reduce abortion and only push thousands of women into "the back alley" where many would be killed or injured. Prohibitions would mean no fewer abortions and more women injured or killed. Wouldn't that be worse than the status quo? Middle America's sense that abortion is a necessary evil explains a lot of things, and, by giving coherent explanation to many disparate facts and impressions, it may provide a way beyond the stalemate to—as Hunter calls for—an elevation in the content and conduct of the public debate.

First, this notion of abortion as a necessary evil explains the seemingly contradictory polls showing that a majority of Americans believe both that abortion is murder and that it should be legal. The most committed pro-life Americans see legality and morality to be inextricably intertwined and therefore view the polling data as contradictory. But Middle America understands "legal" versus "illegal" not in moral terms but in practical terms—criminalizing the procedure. Based on the historical myths, Middle America believes that criminalizing abortion would only aggravate a bad situation.

Second, the myth of abortion as a necessary evil also explains the power of the "choice" rhetoric. For the most committed abortion proponents, "choice" means moral autonomy. But there are less ideological meanings. According to the choice rhetoric, Americans can persuade women to make another choice, but they can't make abortion illegal, because that would mean no fewer abortions and simply push women into the back alley. This explains why Middle America will support virtually any regulation, short of making abortions illegal, that will encourage alternatives and reduce abortions. In a sense, by supporting legal regulations but not prohibitions, many Americans may believe that they are choosing "the lesser of two evils."

Abortion Is Not a Necessary Evil

The rhetoric of abortion as a "necessary evil" (though not the phrase itself) is a key tactic of abortion advocates. It is roughly reflected in President Bill Clinton's slogan that he wants abortion to be "safe, legal, and rare" and is at the heart of Clinton's veto of the federal partial-birth abortion bill. In the face of polls showing that 70 to 80 percent of Americans oppose the procedure, Clinton said that the procedure is horrible (it's an evil) but contends that "a few hundred women" every year must have the procedure (it's necessary).

Indeed, the rhetoric of abortion as a necessary evil is designed to sideline Americans' moral qualms about abortion. For example, when Congress first began to consider the bill prohibiting partial-birth abortion, abortion advocates bought a full-page advertisement in the *New York Times* showing a large coat hanger and the caption, "Will this be the only approved method of abortion?" The coat hanger, reinforcing the image of the back alley, remains a powerful rhetorical symbol. It reinforces the notion that there are two and only two alternatives: abortion on demand or the back alley.

Finally, the myth of abortion as a "necessary evil" also explains why 49 percent of Americans may believe that abortion is "murder" without translating this into fervent social or political mobilization. While Middle Americans may view abortion as an evil, they view it as intractable. For this reason, they view fervent campaigns to prohibit abortion as unrealistic if not counterproductive, while they are drawn to realistic alternatives and regulations. They agree that there are too many abortions and would like to see them reduced. Abortion is not a galvanizing electoral issue for Middle America, because Middle America doesn't see that much can be done about the issue legally or politically.

The Future of Abortion

The myth of abortion as a necessary evil has serious implications for future public debate. First, it means that abortion opponents have won the essential debate that the unborn is a human being and not mere tissue. In fact, the whole thrust of the "choice" argument admits this and seeks to sideline Americans' moral qualms by telling Americans that, even if it is a human life, the most that can be done is to persuade women not to have abortions.

Second, it means that the ideological arguments of both sides ("choice" versus "child") often miss the much more practical concerns of many Americans.

Third, it means that Americans balance the fate of the woman and the fate of the child. Although they understand the fate of the child to be fatal, they want to avoid the same result for women and believe that legalized abortion has been good generally for women.

This means that maximizing the fatal impact of abortion through, for example, graphic pictures of aborted babies is not a "silver bullet" that will transform public opinion alone. Instead, elevating the content and conduct of the public debate requires addressing both aspects—the impact on women as well as the impact on the child. Helping the public understand the impact on both, and the alternatives available, may contribute to a renewal of public dialogue that we so sorely need on this issue.

But a renewal of the public dialogue won't mean much if the people are not allowed to express the public will on this issue, as they usually do in our democratic republic. In 1973, the Supreme Court claimed hegemony over the issue and created a nationwide rule of abortion on demand, preventing democratic debate and solutions. The public policy dictated by the Supreme Court collides with majority opinion and reflects the views of only the 20 percent who are committed to abortion on demand. Twenty-six years later, that is the main reason the pot keeps boiling.

FINDING COMMON GROUND ON ABORTION

Frederica Mathewes-Green

In the following selection, Frederica Mathewes-Green calls for a dialogue between the pro-choice and pro-life sides of the abortion debate. She contends that both sides actually want the same thing: a world without abortion. However, the author asserts, the divisive rhetoric employed by both sides has only served to create misunderstandings and obscure the real issue: finding better solutions to make abortion unnecessary. Mathewes-Green believes that both factions could work together to prevent unintended pregnancies from occurring and to encourage societal changes that would enable more women to choose adoption over abortion. If the abortion debate is engaged from a new angle that searches for areas of agreement and mutually acceptable solutions, she concludes, the real goal—a reduction in abortions—can be achieved. Mathewes-Green is the author of *Real Choices: Listening to Women Looking for Alternatives to Abortion.*

At one point in my life I was pro-choice, but I came over to a pro-life position years ago. I've been there ever since. Perhaps because of my background, I think there's a logic to the pro-choice position that deserves respect, even as we engage it critically. It is possible to disagree with people without calling them baby-killers, without believing that they are monsters or fiends. It is possible to disagree in an agreeable way. The abortion argument is essentially an argument among women. It's been a bitter and ugly debate, and I find that embarrassing.

What the two sides have in common is this: each of us would like to see a world where women no longer want abortions.

Nobody Wants Abortion

I don't believe that even among the most fervent pro-choice people there is anybody who rejoices over abortion. I think we both wish that there were better solutions that could make abortion unnecessary, or prevent pregnancies in the first place. We'd like to see the demand for the procedure reduced, by resolving women's problems and alleviating the pressure for abortion. We can go along this road together as far as we can, and there will come a time when pro-choicers are satisfied and pro-lifers want to keep going, but that doesn't mean we can't go together for now.

A few years ago, quite by accident, I discovered an important piece of common ground. Something I wrote in a conservative think-tank journal was picked up and quoted widely. I had written: "There is a tremendous sadness and loneliness in the cry 'A woman's right to choose.' No one wants an abortion as she wants an ice-cream cone or a Porsche. She wants an abortion as an animal, caught in a trap, wants to gnaw off its own leg."

What surprised me was where it appeared: I started getting clips in the mail from friends, showing the quote featured in pro-choice publications. I realized I had stumbled across one of those points of agreement: we all know that no one leaves the abortion clinic skipping. This made me think that there was common ground, that instead of marching against each other, maybe we could envision a world without abortion, a world we could reach by marching together.

Women and Babies Are Not Enemies

The problem thus far—and I believe the pro-life movement has been especially complicit in this—is that we have focused only on abortion and not on women's needs. We in the pro-life movement have perpetuated a dichotomy where it's the baby against the woman, and we're on the baby's side. You can look over 25 years of pro-life rhetoric and basically boil it down to three words: "It's a baby." We have our little-feet lapel pins, our "Abortion stops a beating heart" bumper stickers, and we've pounded on that message.

In the process we have contributed to what I think is a false concept—an unnatural and even bizarre concept—that women and their unborn children are mortal enemies. We have contributed to the idea that they've got to duke it out, it's going to be a fight to the finish. Either the woman is going to lose control of her life, or the child is going to lose its life.

It occurred to me that there's something wrong with this picture. Nature puts mother and child together; it doesn't make them enemies; it doesn't set one against the other in a battle to the death.

If our rhetoric is tearing them apart, we're the ones who are out of step. When we presume this degree of conflict between women and their own children, we're locating the conflict in the wrong place.

The problem is not located inside women's bodies, it's within society. Social expectations make unwanted pregnancy more likely to occur and harder for women to bear. Unwed mothers are supposed to have abortions, to save the rest of us from all the costs of bringing an "unwanted" child into the world.

Redefining Pro-Life Rhetoric

There are three drawbacks to emphasizing "It's a baby" as the sole message. One is that it contributes to the present deadlock in this debate. We say, "It's a baby," and our friends on the pro-choice side say, "No, it's her right," and the arguments don't even engage each other. It's an endless, interminable argument that can go on for another 25 years if we don't find a way to break through.

Second, the "It's a baby" message alienates the woman distressed by a difficult pregnancy. There's a pro-life message I sometimes hear that makes me cringe: "Women only want abortions for convenience. They do this for frivolous reasons. She wants to fit into her prom dress. She wants to go on a cruise." This alienates the very person to whom we need to show compassion. If we're going to begin finding ways to live without abortion, we need to understand her problems better.

Of course, there has been a wing of the pro-life movement that has been addressing itself to pregnant women's needs for a long time, and that is the crisis-pregnancy-center movement. Centers like these have been giving women maternity clothes, shelter, medical care, job training, and other help for 30 years. I once saw a breakdown of the money and time spent on various sorts of pro-life activities, and over half the movement's energy was going into direct aid to pregnant women. Yet you don't hear this in the rhetoric.

The third problem with this rhetoric is that it enables the people in the great mushy middle, the ones who are neither strongly pro-life nor strongly pro-choice, to go on shrugging off the problem. While both sides know that women don't actually want abortions in any positive sense, the middle is convinced they do.

Pro-lifers say, "She wants an abortion because she's selfish"; pro-choicers say, "She wants an abortion because it will set her free." No wonder the middle believes us: it's one of the few things we appear to agree on.

Both sides know that abortion is usually a very unhappy choice. If women are lining up by the thousands every day to do something they do not want to do, it's not really liberation that women have won. And yet the middle thinks that abortion is what women want, so there's no need for change and nothing to fix.

I can understand why my pro-life allies put the emphasis on "It's a baby." It's a powerful and essential message. Visualizing the violence against the unborn was the conversion point for me and many others. But it cannot be our sole message.

Polls on U.S. attitudes toward abortion show that between 70 and 80 percent already agree that it's a baby—especially since the advent of sonograms. So when we say, "It's a baby," we're answering a question nobody's asking anymore. The real question is, "How could we live without abortion?"

The Unintended Pregnancy Problem

The abortion rate in this country is about 1.5 million a year, a rate that has held fairly stable for about 15 years. Divide that figure by 365 and that equals about 4,000 abortions every day. It's a sobering figure.

The shortsighted pro-life response has been, "Put a padlock on the abortion store." But that's not going to solve the problem. You cannot reduce the demand by shutting off the supply. If 4,000 women were lining up every day to get breast implants, we'd ask, "What's causing this demand? What's going on here?"

Solving the problems that contribute to the demand for abortion will not be easy. The two obvious components are: preventing unwanted pregnancies in the first place, and assisting women who slip through the cracks and become pregnant anyway.

The obvious tool for pregnancy prevention is contraception, but the pro-life movement has been reluctant to support the contraceptive option. Being an Orthodox Christian, I come from a religious tradition that permits some forms of contraception, so it's not been a theological problem for me.

So when I started considering this, I thought, "This is great! I'll get a helicopter, fill it with condoms, get a snow shovel, and just fly over the country tossing 'em out. We'll close all of the abortion clinics tomorrow!"

But then I began to analyze a little deeper. While I believe the pro-life movement needs to make a strong stand in favor of preventing these unplanned pregnancies, I became skeptical of the contraceptive solution.

For example, there's the study showing that about two-thirds of births to teenage moms in California involved a dad who was an adult. Another study found that teen mothers had been forced into sex at a young age and that the men who molested them had an average age of 27.

Closer to home, a friend of mine was brought to an abortion clinic by her older brother, who molested her when she was 12; they gave her a bag of condoms and told her to be more careful. You're not going to solve problems like these by tossing a handful of condoms at them.

But leaving aside the question of sexual abuse, I think we need to look hard at the consequences of the sexual revolution that began in the 1960s. When I entered college in the early 1970s, the revolution was in full bloom. It seemed, at the time, a pretty carefree enterprise. Condoms, pills, and diaphragms were readily available, and abortion had just been legalized by the U.S. Supreme Court.

But I gradually began to think that it was a con game being played on women. We were "expected to behave according to men's notions of sexuality," to use author Adrienne Rich's phrase. Instead of gaining

respect and security in our bodies, we were expected to be more physically available, more vulnerable than before, with little offered in
return.

What women found out is that we have hearts in there along with
all our other physical equipment, and you can't put a condom on
your heart.

So in answering the question "How do we live without abortion?",
I'd say we need to look at restoring respect and righting the balance of
power in male-female sexual relationships.

Women Feeling Alone

What can we do to help women who get pregnant and would rather
not be? For my book *Real Choices*, I went around the country talking to
women who have had an abortion and to women who provide care for
pregnant women. I had presumed that most abortions are prompted
by problems that are financial or practical in nature.

But to my surprise, I found something very different. What I heard
most frequently in my interviews was that the reason for the abortion
was not financial or practical. The core reason I heard was, "I had the
abortion because someone I love told me to." It was either the father
of the child, or else the woman's own mother, who was pressuring her
to have the abortion.

Again and again, I learned that women had abortions because they
felt abandoned—they felt isolated and afraid. As one woman said, "I
felt like everyone would support me if I had the abortion; but if I had
the baby, I'd be alone."

When I asked, "Is there anything anyone could have done? What
would you have needed in order to have had the child?"

I heard the same answer over and over: "I needed a friend. I felt so
alone. I felt like I didn't have a choice. If only one person had stood
by me, even a stranger, I would have had that baby."

The Adoption Option

We also must stop thinking about abortion in terms of pregnancy.
Too often we harp on pregnancy and forget all about what comes
next. Getting through the pregnancy isn't nearly the dilemma that
raising a child for 18 years is. In most families, marriage lightens the
load, but for some people that isn't the best solution. A neglected
option is adoption, which can free the woman to resume her life
while giving the child a loving home.

The numbers on this, however, are shocking. Only 2 percent of
unwed pregnant women choose to place their babies for adoption.
Among clients at crisis-pregnancy centers, it's 1 to 2 percent.

Adoption is a difficult sell to make for a number of complex reasons, but the bottom line is that 80 to 90 percent of the clients who
go through pregnancy care centers and have their babies end by set-

ting up single-parent homes. This is very serious. Pregnancy care centers know this but aren't sure what to do about it.

I, for one, have been strongly encouraging that there be more emphasis on presenting adoption to clients, and equipping center volunteers so they feel comfortable with the topic and enabled to discuss it. Adoption is not a one-size-fits-all solution, but it's got to fit more than 1 or 2 percent. More women should try it on for size.

A Case for Common Ground

In the abortion debate, people are suspicious of looking for any kind of common ground with their adversaries. Why should pro-life partisans—or pro-choicers, for that matter, who feel as strongly about their position as I do about mine—meet together in dialogue? Why should we have anything to do with each other, when the stakes are so high and the convictions so deep?

But common ground does not mean compromise. Compromise is not possible; the alternatives are too stark. Common ground does not have to do with meticulous negotiation whereby, for example, one side gives up partial-birth abortions while the other side gives up RU-486.

In this case, common ground means something more like a demilitarized zone, a safe space where conversation and exploration can take place. It can also refer to those unexpected areas of overlap where both sides find they agree. Imagine two overlapping circles of conviction, one pro-life and one pro-choice. Each circle is complete and has integrity. But there is a space of overlap where beliefs actually coincide—for example, that no one should be forced to have an abortion against her will.

I have been involved in the Common Ground Network for Life and Choice for several years, and can only bear witness from my own life. In light of the deadlocked, rancorous, poisonous quality of much of this debate, the appearance of Common Ground has been a healing, hopeful experience for me. And I dare hope that one day we may actually see solutions.

Common Ground is, at root, people talking. It's been a spontaneous impulse arising in a dozen cities or so across the country since the early 1990s: Denver, Buffalo, Cleveland, Washington. Eventually the various groups linked up through an umbrella organization we call the Common Ground Network for Life and Choice, with Washington headquarters.

Understanding Both Sides

While Common Ground isn't for everyone, I believe it is a movement that promises to season the abortion debate with patience, consideration, and respect—something the present mudwrestling sorely needs.

One of the reasons why I participate in Common Ground is curiosity. Don't you ever wonder, "What are those people on the other side thinking? What makes them tick?" In our local group, we take turns asking questions like, "Will contraception and sex education reduce the numbers of abortions?" and "What are the acceptable limits of protest outside of abortion clinics?" In fact, two Common Grounders, an Operation Rescue leader and the administrator of an abortion clinic, are planning to write a joint paper on that very question.

Another sort of curiosity is born of frustration. I am frustrated by the deadlock on this issue, by the intractability of it, and simply want to take a crack at coming at it from a new angle—like the toddler sitting at a computer keyboard and thinking, "I wonder what will happen if I push this button?"

Sometimes, just trying something new because you're frustrated with the old can lead to disaster. But I cannot see any danger in Common Ground dialogues. Pro-lifers, at least, have nothing to lose, because we have nothing: the status quo lies with the other side, with court decisions to hold it in place.

Through my participation in Common Ground, I also hope to eliminate misunderstanding and replace it with genuine disagreement.

I'm not naive enough to believe that our divisions are superficial, and that if we could only chat them away it would be all hugs and kisses. But misunderstanding—genuine confusion about what your opponent believes and what motivates her—is a waste of time.

I know I get weary of being told I'm pro-life because I'm sexist, or antisex, or want women to be restricted to breeding and not allowed to have careers or carry cell phones. This fantasy is untrue. If pro-choicers truly understood what motivates me, I don't think they would like it much better, but at least they would not be going on bogeyman stories.

Likewise, pro-choicers must get weary of being told they're "pro-abortion" because it makes them so much money, that they don't care about children and families, and are elite godless commie pinko perverts to boot. I'd like to diffuse our absurd misunderstandings, so we can get down to grappling with the honest disagreements underneath.

Finding Out the Facts

I also like to talk about a related point I call data block versus ideo block. Sometimes our conflict is honestly based in different beliefs or ideologies: we are looking at the same reality (for example, the abortion of an infant with Down's syndrome) and simply disagree about what constitutes right or wrong.

In other cases, however, we disagree about what the facts are in the first place—our communication is experiencing a data block, not an ideology block.

One side, for example, tends to believe that better sex education and access to contraception will reduce the numbers of abortions. The other side tends to believe that, under a principle of unintended consequences, these items actually increase the likelihood of unwed pregnancy.

Which is true? Each side can marshal a barrage of facts to support its theory, but it's like swimming in soup—too many details, not enough certainty.

If one theory or the other could be proved true, the dissenting side might be persuaded. Both sides are looking for ways to reduce the numbers of abortions; we have a shared goal. We're just in disagreement about whether contraception will get us there, because we're holding different sets of facts.

One project the Common Ground Network has discussed is establishing a data bank of facts that both sides agree on. We could start with basics: how many abortions per year or when the fetal heartbeat begins. Trickier questions we could refer to organizations on both sides of the issue—and whenever we discover agreement, we could add it to the list. Gradually a data bank could grow, which would serve as a resource to journalists, students, and other researchers and contribute to clearing the air. A glossary might also be useful.

Solving Problems Together

Common Ground allows us to scout out areas far from the hot center, where agreement may already exist. We've found, for example, a common interest in making adoption a more accessible option and raising the profile of that alternative. We've agreed on the urgency of reducing unwed teen pregnancy, and that it's wrong to use violence outside of clinics.

By continually putting our heads together in Common Ground, I keep hoping we'll find fresh ways of understanding the problem. I hope that informal and friendly links forged across the great divide can grow, over time, from rope bridges to giant trestles linking continents. But even now the power of networking is astonishing. All of us together have resources that neither of us has alone.

A few years ago, for example, the Reproductive Health Services clinic in St. Louis, Missouri was faced with an extremely young client who was too far along to have an abortion. This girl needed to be on complete bed rest to safely finish her pregnancy and needed someone to stay with her all day while her mother worked.

The clinic did not have the resources to collect a roster of volunteers for this duty. The clinic administrator, a member of the local Common Ground group, then phoned a pro-lifer in the group, a woman who had been arrested leading protests outside the clinic. The pro-lifer was able to enlist a cohort of volunteers from the pro-life community, and the girl was able to safely complete her pregnancy.

If the pro-choice and pro-life communities had been locked in the sort of armed warfare seen in most cities, the side that had the resources—in this case, the pro-life side—might never have known that the other side had a need. The more we get to know each other, the more suspicious fear can evaporate, and the more likely we are to find opportunities to actually make a difference.

The Advantages of Dialogue

Being in Common Ground has eased my heart. I have found that having a pro-choicer listen intently to my beliefs, then repeat them back to me accurately, is healing.

I believe I now have a much better understanding of how things stand from the pro-choice point of view, too. My views haven't changed; I still believe that their position is wrong. But my listening, for example, has taught me how much a phrase like "abortion kills babies" hurts many who hold a pro-choice position. To pro-lifers, it's just a forceful statement of fact; but I've discovered that pro-choicers almost inevitably hear, "I think you personally like killing babies." So I try to express my feelings on this without implying that those who disagree are callous or depraved. They're not. They're just wrong.

Likewise, the phrase "anti-choice" hits me like a slap in the face. I'm not easily angered, but being called "anti-choice" makes me see red. Yes, I don't believe that taking a life is an appropriate private choice. But when I'm called "anti-choice," I feel like I'm being told I'm a fascist, and that if I had my way people wouldn't be allowed to choose anything—hair color, make of car, what they'll have for supper. I think my pro-choice friends, who use it interchangeably with "anti-abortion" and "pro-life," probably don't realize how it stings. Seeing things from the other's point of view is one of the advantages of dialogue.

I also participate in Common Ground because I am committed to a consistent ethic of valuing all human life and rejecting violence as a means of solving social problems. Cardinal Joseph Bernardin, of blessed memory, gave the nation a gift when he defined the moral principle that underlies this ethic as a "seamless garment": the consistent opposition to war, abortion, and capital punishment. Not all pro-lifers view these three forms of death-dealing as morally equivalent, but it's the view that appeals most to me. In any case, all pro-lifers would say that abortion is the most urgent of these three, the only one taking 4,000 lives a day in this country.

As I root out of my life a spirit of violence at deeper and deeper levels, I come face to face with Jesus' command to love my enemies. It's because I've uncovered a startling fact: it wasn't until I became a pro-life activist that, for the first time in my life, I had actual enemies. Realizing that I had them, I knew then what I had to do—after all, the scriptural instruction on this is not vague.

I also think of another scripture passage, the one that says you cannot love your brother whom you have not seen. So I think that's the least I can do: to go see them, on a regular basis. True, the Common Ground movement is not the sort that sweeps the country, generating

TV ads, political candidates, Hollywood parties, and T-shirt slogans. But it's the sort of movement that, I hope, can begin to subtly disrupt entrenched patterns of mistrust and loathing.

If pro-lifers and pro-choicers ripped off the scary masks we've imposed on each other, we would discover that underneath there are sincere people who, astonishingly, have the same goal: reducing the heartbreakingly high number of abortions. Both know that 4,000 abortions a day is too many. We can harness that agreement for positive change, leaving those areas where we disagree for action within our own sides.

CHAPTER 4

WOMEN'S RIGHTS AROUND THE WORLD

CREATING CHANGE FROM WITHIN ISLAMIC CULTURE

Nicole Gaouette

Many Westerners believe that women in Islamic countries suffer under brutal oppression, symbolized by the veils they are required to wear in public. However, as Nicole Gaouette shows, Islamic women themselves see the veil as the least of their problems. According to the author, most women who live under strict Islamic regimes would like to gain more rights, but only in the context of their own culture. Gaouette finds that many Muslim women are offended by clichéd Western perceptions of who they are or what changes they should seek. They insist that they have many of the same problems as Western women, she writes, including trying to balance work and family. Islamic women are attempting to create cultural change from the inside, Gaouette reports, tackling issues such as child custody and inheritance laws. They are also working to change attitudes toward women's access to education, employment, and travel. Based in Saudi Arabia, Gaouette is a staff writer for the *Christian Science Monitor*.

If there is a Western shorthand for Muslim women, it might look like Heba Attieh.

Veiled and cautious about encounters with men outside her Saudi family, she was married at 17 to someone she barely knew. Soon after, she was pregnant with the first of three children. She can't travel in Saudi Arabia without a man's permission, leave the house alone, or drive.

But look again.

Ms. Attieh, tall, slim, with an easy sense of humor, is also a doctor at King Faisal Specialist Hospital in Jeddah, Saudi Arabia, where she works full time alongside male colleagues.

She holds a PhD in speech pathology, does community work, and is organizing a group to work on school-curriculum issues and playground development.

"How many Western women do as much?" challenges her sister-in-law, Sahar Abdul Majid.

Veils Are Not the Problem

In these days of tension between Islam and the West, it's a question that resonates with many Muslim women. The US war against Afghanistan's Taliban regime has put Islam front and center in the American consciousness. Some of the most popular news reports are about Afghan women reclaiming their jobs, their studies, and their right to remove the head-to-toe burqa covering.

To many Westerners these moments are ripe with symbolism: In their eyes, the veil reflects Islam's oppression of women. Some commentators have even hailed the liberation of Afghanistan's women. "Muslim women see it in a slightly different light," Attieh wryly observes.

It is too early to tell how events will play out for Afghanistan's women. But the fall of the Taliban leaves just two countries—Saudi Arabia and Iran—that dictate, by law, that women cover themselves. For outsiders who hold that Muslim women need freeing from the shackles of their faith, these would be the countries to turn to next. Most Iranian and Saudi women, though, won't be having any of it. Despite differences of geography, culture, and language, the women of these two countries echo each other's tart appraisals of the West and its view of Muslim women.

They bridle at Western assumptions about the nature of Islam and a woman's place in it. Like their Afghan sisters, these women stress that culture shapes their lives as much as religion and if they have problems, the veil certainly isn't one of them. They want change, but on terms that suit their society. Most of all, they would like Westerners to stop rehashing old clichés about who they are.

"Talk to us, see us," says Attieh in a hospital room brightened with children's drawings. "It's true we may not have many rights. But we deal with the same problems you do—juggling jobs and kids, finding some balance and a place for ourselves. A lot of people here want change, we just have to do it in a way that works with our culture, not against it."

The Women of Afghanistan

In the lush green courtyard of Shafiqa's family home in Jalalabad, Afghanistan, a half-dozen highly educated women are doing what they have done for the past five years: laughing, gossiping, and raising their children.

None of these sisters and cousins—doctors, teachers, and professionals—has ventured outside their home in that time. Husbands, brothers, and fathers do the grocery shopping, they say, though not very well.

The Taliban may have left Jalalabad now, replaced by mujahideen guerrillas loosely aligned with the Northern Alliance, but Shafiqa and her relatives say they still will not leave their homes without a veil.

"In our culture, it is necessary to wear a scarf and [long] sleeves," says Shafiqa, a medical-school graduate. Another reason for her caution, she says, is that the new rulers of Jalalabad are just as conservative—and perhaps less law-abiding—than the Taliban.

Few Afghan women forget that the Northern Alliance organized campaigns of rape against women of different ethnic backgrounds before the Taliban took over. "People are not safe because the mujahideen are just like the Taliban," Shafiqa says.

Following Islamic Law

In some places, the departure of the Taliban means a return to freedoms that Afghan women enjoyed before—to work, study, and move at will. In more traditional areas, where most of Afghanistan's 25 million people live, the change is more modest, as ancient customs replace strict Taliban laws.

In the cool shade of a tree, a farmer named Sher Jan and his wife, Rahmona, reflect on their lives since the Taliban's departure. They get sidetracked easily by gentle differences of opinion. She corrects him when he says they have three children. ("Yes, we have three boys, but we also have four girls," she says.) And he corrects her on her age. ("Forty," she says. "Fifty," he says.)

But on one subject, the couple speaks in harmony. The Taliban were enforcing Islamic laws that most Muslims already obeyed. "To wear a burqa, this is the instruction of the holy Prophet Muhammad and they made it obligatory, as if almighty God said it," says Sher Jan. The Taliban had good intentions and made the city safe for women, says Rahmona, but occasionally, out of zealotry, the Taliban themselves became harassers.

"One day, I was forced to get down by the Taliban from a bullock cart," she recalls. Reflexively, she pulls her black scarf across her face in the presence of a male stranger. "They told me, you should wear the burqa. I told them, I'm too old to wear a burqa. Eventually, they let me go."

It is midnight in Jeddah, and in Neda Hariri's plush living room the conversation is just picking up steam. During the holy month of Ramadan, Muslims fast all day and socialize late into the night, and Attieh has come to visit her niece and sister-in-law.

Out of her hospital whites, Attieh is coolly elegant in a gray linen suit. Ms. Hariri, newly married and pregnant, is still slender in a silk tank top and skirt. As she hands around cake and sweets, her mother whispers hostessing advice.

But when talk turns to Afghanistan, tips on serving implements are forgotten as the women start discussing Western reports on Afghan women and the veil. "You have to understand that most of these [Afghan] women want to cover their head," interjects Attieh. "They have no malls, no Internet, there is just religion. The veil is a symbol of faith, a form of protection, like a second skin."

Hariri complains about first lady Laura Bush's radio address in November 2001 on Afghan women, arguing that it was meant to provide the US with an excuse to keep bombing. "It's not for women in the US to say Afghan women are oppressed and should take off the veil," she says. "If an Afghan woman is upset about her situation, she should change it, not you."

Using Women to Justify Foreign Interference

History gives her good reason to be suspicious. European nations often used Muslim women to justify their intrusions into Islamic countries. In the late 1800s, the English envoy Evelyn Baring urged his superiors to colonize Egypt, arguing they could do so on behalf of the country's downtrodden women. At the time, Baring sat on a committee bent on denying English women the vote.

French charities in late 19th-century Algeria would dispense free oil and flour to the poor, but only if they removed their veils. "[Mrs. Bush's] speech resonates so much with this earlier use of women as a reason to interfere in internal affairs," observes Barbara Petzen, a historian at Harvard University in Cambridge, Mass. "Before Sept. 11, there wasn't much Western interest in Afghan women. The Islamic world was much more vocal about Taliban practices."

The misgivings aren't confined to Hariri's living room. Iran Aflatouni, a retired computer programmer in Tehran, doubts the West's understanding of Afghan women. "Even if women are liberated from Taliban rule, they have a culture that does not accept women as equals to men," she says.

Iranians have their own reasons to distrust Western interference. The US toppled a democratically elected Iranian government in the 1950s to put the shah in power. Iranians endured the shah's brutal secret police and while he instituted changes for women, his attempt to graft Western-style reforms onto Iranian culture wasn't a success.

So many families felt Iranian society was immoral that some experts estimate that up to 50 percent of young women were kept from university. For these women, the 1979 Islamic revolution was a liberation. They could study, work and become a public force. Women now take 60 percent of university places.

Today, Iran's hardline Islamic clerics present a stumbling block for women as they vigorously block attempts at political and social reform. Crackdowns on women's dress often represent the clerics' resistance to larger kinds of social change. In Saudi Arabia, too, religious conservatives make women a scapegoat when fighting off change of any kind.

Despite the obstacles thrown up in the name of religion, many Iranians still see the revolution as a blessing.

"People from the outside, when they look at us, they just see the small percentage like me who have gone under the [veil]," says Negar

Eskandarfar, the publisher of a Tehran literary magazine. "They don't see that huge percentage who have come out into society from inside their houses, from the back rooms, from illiteracy."

Testing Islamic Law

The Western preoccupation with the veil puzzles many women. "Iranian women have far more important issues than the veil," says Aflatouni. "Our laws are backward."

Courts deny Iranian women child custody after divorce, which men get more easily. Women are considered half a witness and are entitled to only half what their male siblings inherit. They need a male guardian's permission to travel abroad and must cope with the basij, the morality police who enforce proper Islamic behavior and dress.

Saudi women have their own religious police and similar legal hurdles, but in both countries women are working the gap between law and attitude.

In Iran, this is most colorfully expressed through clothing. Since the revolution, women's clothing has cycled through political as well as fashion seasons. Women test the political boundaries by shortening their coats, letting more hair show under their scarves and dusting their faces with a light bloom of makeup. After government crackdowns, coats get longer, and hair is carefully tucked away.

Saudi women have even less flexibility with dress, so challenges to the status quo are less visible. But there are middle-class women who presage change and Nadia Baeshen is one of them. She runs her own Jeddah-based consulting company, heads the women's business department at a local university and teaches at two women's colleges.

"There are certain rules you have to follow, but once you're out there, you're out there," she says. "Just don't defy the system and no one cares what you do." Seated in her office in black jeans and a funky black-and-white jacket, Ms. Baeshen projects a sharp intelligence. She dismisses travel permits as a technicality, doesn't bother with all-women banks, and says her gender is a plus.

"My American friends don't believe it, but being a woman in my culture is very advantageous," she says. "In the men's bank, everyone lets me go to the front of the line. People give women some leeway and lots of respect."

She sees a silver lining in the ban on women driving. Like most women of means, she uses a driver, most of whom come from abroad to work for a few hundred dollars a month. "I do all my phone calls, set up appointments and I don't have to worry about parking," Baeshen says. "Is that so bad by American standards?"

She doesn't say how she deals with the requirement that women appoint a male proxy to conduct their business in the public arena, at government offices for instance. But some women pay a man to fill the role on paper, then take care of public business themselves.

Changing Attitudes Toward Women

Women without Baeshen's means may have a harder time, but change is filtering down the socioeconomic ladder, says Abubaker A. Bagader, a sociology professor at Jeddah's King Abdul Aziz University. Travel, satellite TV, and the Internet provide some impetus for change, but much of it comes from within, he says.

While Saudi Arabia is one of the wealthiest Muslim nations, it has one of the lowest female labor rates in the Middle East. Its literacy rate among women lags behind Egypt, Algeria, and Libya. But Saudi Arabia has also undergone a huge rural-urban shift. Sixty percent of the population is now under age 20, and live in nuclear families. As attitudes change, more women are being educated. In a 1990 survey, Mr. Bagader found 80 percent of men wanted a college-educated wife, up from just over 50 percent in 1979. Very slowly, more women are working—out of necessity as much as by choice—as a lackluster economy squeezes incomes.

Fatin Bundagji, director of Women's Training Programs at Jeddah's Chamber of Commerce, helps women polish their skills for the job market, but with so few places available it can be discouraging work. "A friend of mine at a government office has 90,000 women's resumes," she says. "Where are these women now? Where do girls go when they graduate? Nowhere. And I'm educating them even further to go nowhere. It really saddens me."

It is almost 2 A.M. and the discussion in Neda Hariri's living room is still going strong. Her mother, Mrs. Abdul Majid, is complaining about the requirement that women get male permission to travel. "Some [Islamic] scholars say no, you don't need it," she fumes. "I think it's just wrong." When Saudi women talk about restrictions that chafe, they sometimes point out that the Islamic basis for the rule is debatable if not invisible. More often than not they point to culture as the impediment to being more politically active or more mobile.

Attieh says the answer lies in creating change within the culture. And if women are stereotypically confined to the spheres of home, children, and schooling, she says that can be a strength. "There is great potential for change and social power there," she says. "Cultural rules change with time. Just look at your mother's life and your own."

Some, though not many, say Attieh has a silent partner in the government. In Jeddah, it has backed the recent creation of two new women's colleges and set up a national employment and training project. And it recently began issuing Saudi women their own identification card, instead of a paper that only identified them by their male guardian. Some women see this as a step toward allowing women to drive. "The government is on the side of women," insists a male media analyst. "But it's held captive to the [religious conservatives]."

Women Will Gain More Power

A crackdown on Saudi women followed the Gulf War, when critics say the government moved to appease religious conservatives angry about the stationing of US troops on Saudi soil. Some worry that this may happen again, in the wake of the Sept. 11 attacks on the US and its subsequent war on Afghanistan.

But even so, women and analysts say change is simply a matter of time. Iran's women have voting power. And like Iranians, Saudi women are becoming increasingly well educated, a point observers stress strongly. "Watch what educated Muslim women do," says Elizabeth Warnock Fernea, an American writer and filmmaker who focuses on Middle Eastern women and the family. "They will be a force to be reckoned with."

Hariri, who dropped her university studies when she got pregnant, plans to go back one day. Looking ahead to her long-term hopes and goals, she starts thinking aloud, her kohl-rimmed eyes fixed in the distance. More freedom, she says, the ability to drive and choose a profession, the chance to vote and be politically active. "Because I'm a human being and I should have my freedom," she says, snapping back into focus. "Especially from my husband's family," she adds, and the room around her echoes her laugh.

UNMASKING THE TRADITION OF FEMALE CIRCUMCISION

Rogaia Mustafa Abusharaf

The following selection by Sudanese-born anthropologist Rogaia Mustafa Abusharaf discusses the tradition of ritualized genital surgeries performed on young girls and women in some areas of Africa and Asia. While the notion of removing part of a woman's genitals seems barbaric from a Western perspective, the author points out that in many communities this practice is an important tradition that dates back more than one thousand years. On the other hand, the author writes, there are many negative health effects associated with female circumcision, such as infections, complications with pregnancy, and even death. If female genital cutting is to be abolished, Abusharaf believes, Westerners need to understand and work with the cultural beliefs that surround it. Ultimately, the impetus for change must come from within the communities that practice female circumcision. Abusharaf is a visiting scholar at the Pembroke Center for Teaching and Research on Women at Brown University in Providence, Rhode Island.

I will never forget the day of my circumcision, which took place forty years ago. I was six years old. One morning during my school summer vacation, my mother told me that I had to go with her to her sisters' house and then to visit a sick relative in Halfayat El Mulook [in the northern part of Khartoum, Sudan]. We did go to my aunts' house, and from there all of us went straight to [a] red brick house [I had never seen].

While my mother was knocking, I tried to pronounce the name on the door. Soon enough I realized that it was Hajja Alamin's house. She was the midwife who performed circumcisions on girls in my neighhorhood. I was petrified and tried to break loose. But I was captured and subdued by my mother and two aunts. They began to tell me that the midwife was going to purify me.

The midwife was the cruelest person I had seen . . . [She] ordered her young maid to go buy razors from the Yemeni grocer next door. I still remember her when she came back with the razors, which were enveloped in purple wrapping with a crocodile drawing on it.

The women ordered me to lie down on a bed [made of ropes] that had a hole in the middle. They held me tight while the midwife started to cut my flesh without anesthetics. I screamed till I lost my voice. The midwife was saying to me, "Do you want me to be taken into police custody?" After the job was done I could not eat, drink or even pass urine for three days. I remember one of my uncles who discovered what they did to me threatened to press charges against his sisters. They were afraid of him and they decided to bring me back to the midwife. In her sternest voice she ordered me to squat on the floor and urinate. It seemed like the most difficult thing to do at that point, but I did it. I urinated for a long time and was shivering with pain.

It took a very long time [before] I was back to normal. I understand the motives of my mother, that she wanted me to be clean, but I suffered a lot.

—from a 1989 interview with Aisha Abdel Majid, a Sudanese woman working as a teacher in the Middle East

A Coming-of-Age Ritual

Aisha Abdel Majid's story echoes the experience of millions of African women who have undergone ritualized genital surgeries, often as young girls, without anesthesia, in unsanitary conditions, the surgical implement a knife, a razor blade or a broken bottle wielded by a person with no medical training. The pain and bleeding are intense; the girls sometimes die. Survivors are prone to a host of medical complications that can plague them throughout their lives, including recurrent infections, pain during intercourse, infertility and obstructed labor that can cause babies to be born dead or brain-damaged.

Female circumcision, also known as genital mutilation, is a common practice in at least twenty-eight African countries, cutting a brutal swath through the center of the continent—from Mauritania and the Ivory Coast in the west to Egypt, Somalia and Tanzania in the east. The ritual also takes place among a few ethnic groups in Asia. Where it is practiced, female circumcision is passionately perpetuated and closely safeguarded; it is regarded as an essential coming-of-age ritual that ensures chastity, promotes cleanliness and fertility, and enhances the beauty of a woman's body. In Arabic the colloquial word for circumcision, *tahara*, means "to purify." It is estimated that between 100 million and 130 million women living today have undergone genital surgeries, and each year two million more—mostly girls from four to twelve years old—will be cut.

In December 1997 genital mutilation became illegal in Egypt, thanks to a closely watched court decision, and women's groups in Africa and abroad hope that the landmark ruling will bolster eradication efforts worldwide. But most people working for change recognize that government action, though an important and useful symbol, is ultimately not the answer. Barbaric though the ritual may seem to Westerners, female circumcision is deeply enmeshed in local traditions and beliefs. Treating it as a crime and punishing offenders with jail time would in many cases be unfair. Mothers who bring their daughters for the operation believe they are doing the right thing—and indeed, their children would likely become social outcasts if left uncut. You cannot arrest an entire village.

Make no mistake: I believe that genital mutilation must end if women are to enjoy the most basic human rights. But it does little good for a Westerner, or even an African-born woman such as myself, to condemn the practice unilaterally. We must learn from history: when colonial European powers tried to abolish the surgery in the first half of the twentieth century, local people rejected the interference and clung even more fiercely to their traditions. Without an understanding of indigenous cultures, and without a deep commitment from within those cultures to end the cutting, eradication efforts imposed from the outside are bound to fail. Nothing highlights the problem more clearly than the two terms used to describe the procedure: is it circumcision, an "act of love," as some women call it, or mutilation? Contradictory though the answer might seem, it is both.

The Justifications for Genital Cutting

Because genital cutting is considered an essential aspect of a woman's identity, abolishing it has profound social implications. Think of the politics and emotions in Western countries that have swirled around issues such as abortion, the right of homosexuals to be parents and the ethics of human cloning. Any change that requires a readjustment of long-established social mores makes people highly uncomfortable.

The justifications for female circumcision vary. Some ethnic groups in Nigeria believe that if a woman's clitoris is not removed, contact with it will kill a baby during childbirth. Other people believe that, unchecked, the female genitalia will continue to grow, becoming a grotesque penislike organ dangling between a woman's legs. Vaginal secretions, produced by glands that are often removed as part of the surgery, are thought to be unclean and lethal to sperm.

Circumcision is also intended to dull women's sexual enjoyment, and to that end it is chillingly effective. In a survey conducted in Sierra Leone, circumcised women reported feeling little or no sexual responsiveness. The clitoris is always at least partially removed during the operation, and without it orgasm becomes practically impossible.

Killing women's desire is thought to keep them chaste; in fact, genital cutting is so closely associated with virginity that a girl who is spared the ordeal by enlightened parents is generally assumed to be promiscuous, a man-chaser.

Such beliefs may seem absurd to outsiders. But in the nineteenth century respected doctors in England and the United States performed clitoridectomies on women as a supposed "cure" for masturbation, nymphomania and psychological problems. Today some girls and women in the West starve themselves obsessively. Others undergo painful and potentially dangerous medical procedures—face lifts, liposuction, breast implants and the like—to conform to cultural standards of beauty and femininity. I am not trying to equate genital cutting with eating disorders or cosmetic surgery; nevertheless, people in the industrialized world must recognize that they too are influenced, often destructively, by traditional gender roles and demands.

Genital Surgery and Its Complications

Local custom determines which kind of genital surgery girls undergo. Part or all of the clitoris may be removed; that is called clitoridectomy. A second kind of operation is excision, in which the clitoris and part or all of the labia minora, the inner lips of the vagina, are cut away. Clitoridectomy and excision are practiced on the west coast of Africa, in Chad and the Central African Republic, and in Kenya and Tanzania.

The most drastic form of genital surgery is infibulation, in which the clitoris and labia minora are removed, and then the labia majora, the outer lips of the vagina, are stitched together to cover the urethral and vaginal entrances. The goal is to make the genital area a blank patch of skin. A Sudanese woman in her sixties I interviewed told me that the midwife performing the surgery is often reminded by a girl's kinswomen to "make it smooth and beautiful like the back of a pigeon." A new opening is created for the passage of urine and menstrual blood and for sex—but the opening is made small, to increase the man's enjoyment. After the operation a girl's legs may be tied together for weeks so that skin grows over the wound. Women who have undergone infibulation must be cut open before childbirth and restitched afterward. Infibulation is practiced in Mali, Sudan, Somalia and parts of Ethiopia and northern Nigeria.

Genital surgery is usually performed by a midwife, either at her home, in the girl's home or in some cases in a special hut where a group of girls is sequestered during the initiation period. Midwives often have no medical training and little anatomical knowledge; if a girl struggles or flinches from the pain, the surgical instrument may slip, causing additional damage. There is also concern that unsterilized circumcision instruments may be spreading the AIDS virus. Among affluent Africans there is a growing trend to have the operation performed by physicians in private clinics—sometimes as far away as Europe—where general anesthesia is administered and conditions are hygienic.

The word *circumcision* (literally, "cutting around"), which was borrowed from the male operation, is a striking misnomer when applied to the procedures performed on women. Male circumcision, in which the foreskin of the penis is removed, is not associated with health problems, nor does it interfere with sexual functioning or enjoyment. By contrast, the immediate complications of female genital surgery include tetanus and other infections, severe pain, and hemorrhaging, which can in turn lead to shock and death. In July 1996 the Western press reported that an eleven-year-old Egyptian girl had died following a circumcision performed by a barber. The following month a fourteen-year-old girl died, also in Egypt. Countless other deaths go unreported.

Long-term complications of genital surgery are also common, particularly for women who have been infibulated. Scar tissue blocking the urethral or vaginal opening can lead to a buildup of urine and menstrual blood, which, in turn, can cause chronic pelvic and urinary-tract infections. The infections can lead to back pain, kidney damage, severe uterine cramping and infertility. If sebaceous glands in the skin become embedded in the stitched area during the surgery, cysts the size of grapefruits may form along the scar. Nerve endings can also become entrapped in the scar, causing extreme pain during sex.

Childbirth poses many special dangers for the infibulated woman. The baby's head may push through the perineum, the muscular area between the vagina and the anus. Sometimes a fistula, or abnormal passage, between the bladder and the vagina develops because of damage caused by obstructed labor. Women who develop fistulas may suffer frequent miscarriages because of urine seeping into the uterus. In addition, they smell of urine and often become outcasts.

Not surprisingly, depression and anxiety are also frequent consequences of genital surgery—whether spurred by health problems, fears of infertility or the loss of a husband's attention because of penetration difficulties.

Circumcision and Social Status

In spite of its grim nature, female circumcision is cloaked in festivity. Girls are feted and regaled with gifts after the operation. In some societies the experience includes secret ceremonies and instruction in cooking, crafts, child care and the use of herbs. After circumcision adolescent girls suddenly become marriageable, and they are allowed to wear jewelry and womanly garments that advertise their charms. Among the Masai of Kenya and Tanzania, girls undergo the operation publicly; then the cutting becomes a test of bravery and a proof that they will be able to endure the pain of childbirth. Circumcision gives girls status in their communities. By complying, they also please their parents, who can arrange a marriage and gain a high bridal price for a circumcised daughter.

The consequences of not undergoing the ritual are equally powerful: teasing, disrespect and ostracism. Among the Sabiny people of Uganda, an uncircumcised woman who marries into the community is always lowest in the pecking order of village women, and she is not allowed to perform the public duties of a wife, such as serving elders. Uncut women are called girls, whatever their age, and they are forbidden to speak at community gatherings. The social pressures are so intense that uncircumcised wives often opt for the operation as adults.

Girls, too, can be driven to desperation. A Somali woman identified as Anab was quoted in a report by a local women's group:

> When girls of my age were looking after the lambs, they would talk among themselves about their circumcision experiences and look at each other's genitals to see who had the smallest opening. Every time the other girls showed their infibulated genitals, I would feel ashamed I was not yet circumcised. Whenever I touched the hair of infibulated girls, they would tell me not to touch them since I was [still] "unclean." . . . One day I could not stand it anymore. I took a razor blade and went to an isolated place. I tied my clitoris with a thread, and while pulling at the thread with one hand I tried to cut part of my clitoris. When I felt the pain and saw the blood coming from the cut I stopped. . . . I was seven years old.

Yet despite the peer pressure and the benefits to be gained from being circumcised, the prospect of the operation can loom threateningly over a girl's childhood, poisoning everyday activities and filling her with fear and suspicion. Memuna M. Sillah, a New York City college student who grew up in Sierra Leone, described in a recent story in *Natural History* how as a child, whenever her mother sent her on an unusual errand, she feared that it might be a trick, that this might be the moment when strange women would grab her and cut her flesh. And Taha Baashar, a Sudanese psychologist, has reported the case of a seven-year-old girl who suffered from insomnia and hallucinations caused by fear of the operation. The problems reportedly improved when the girl was promised she would not be circumcised.

Historical Origins

The origins of female circumcision are uncertain. Folk wisdom associates it with ancient Egypt, though the examination of mummies has so far provided no corroboration. Ancient Egyptian myths stressed the bisexuality of the gods, and so circumcision may have been introduced to clarify the femininity of girls. (In some African countries the clitoris is considered a masculine organ, and in the fetus, of course, both clitoris and penis develop from the same precursor tissue.) At any rate, the ritual certainly dates back more than 1,000 years: the eighth-century poet El Farazdaq denounced the tribe of Azd in the Arabian peninsula in one of his lampoons, writing that their women had never experienced the pain of circumcision and were therefore "of inferior stock."

Although female circumcision is practiced by Africans of all religions—Muslims, Christians and Ethiopian Jews, as well as followers of animist religions, such as the Masai—it is particularly associated with Islam. Many Muslims believe the ritual is a religious obligation. In fact, however, female circumcision is not mentioned in the Koran, and it is unknown in predominantly Muslim countries outside of Africa, such as Saudi Arabia and Iraq. What seems likely is that when Islam came to Africa, its emphasis on purity became associated with the existing practice of genital cutting—much the way early Christianity assimilated existing pagan rituals such as decorating evergreen trees.

Female circumcision came to European attention long ago. An early historical record can be found in the writings of Pietro Bembo, the sixteenth-century Italian cardinal:

> They now . . . sailed into the Red Sea and visited several areas inhabited by blacks, excellent men, brave in war. Among these people the private parts of the girls are sewn together immediately after birth, but in a way not to hinder the urinary ways. When the girls have become adults, they are given away in marriage in this condition and the husbands' first measure is to cut open with a knife the solidly consolidated private parts of the virgin. Among the barbarous people virginity is held in high esteem.

Other Europeans also wrote about genital cutting in accounts that were read by generations of foreign travelers to Africa. But despite some attempts by Christian missionaries and colonial powers to intervene, genital mutilation remained largely unknown abroad until the 1950s, when nationalist struggles gave rise to the women's movement in Africa. It was then that local activists and medical professionals began publicly condemning the practice.

Fighting to Abolish Genital Mutilation

After college I lived in Khartoum and worked for two years at a development corporation. A secretary I became friendly with there, whom I will call Shadia, confided in me that she found intercourse painful because of the effects of her circumcision. She and her husband had agreed, she told me, that any daughters of theirs would not be cut.

In 1996 I returned to Sudan to visit friends, and I looked up Shadia. We had not seen each other for a decade. We embraced; I asked about her children and she pulled out a photograph. I gasped. The three girls, the youngest of whom was about six, were dressed in jewelry and fancy clothes, their hands and feet patterned with henna, and around their shoulders they wore traditional maroon-and-gold satin shawls called *firkas*. It was unmistakably a picture from a circumcision celebration. How could my friend have had such a change of heart? I was shocked.

Shadia explained. One day while she was at work her mother-in-law, who lived with the family, had secretly taken the girls to be circumcised, in defiance of their parents' wishes. When Shadia's husband, a truck driver, returned home, he was so distraught that he left the house and did not return for a week. Shadia was also heartbroken but she consoled herself that the girls had "only" been given clitoridectomies; at least they had not been infibulated, as she had. "It could have been worse," she told me resignedly.

Entrenched customs die hard, and the task facing anticircumcisionists is daunting. They can take heart, however, from the precedents: foot binding and widow burning, once widespread in China and India, respectively, have been abolished.

International efforts to end genital mutilation began in 1979, when the World Health Organization published statements against it. Then, after a gathering of African women's organizations in Dakar, Senegal, in 1984, the Inter-African Committee Against Traditional Practices Affecting the Health of Women and Children was formed; since then, affiliates in twenty-three African countries have been working to end the practice. In 1994 the International Conference on Population and Development in Cairo adopted the first international document to specifically address female genital mutilation, calling it a "basic rights violation" that should be prohibited.

A variety of projects have aimed to end genital cutting:

• *Alternative initiation rituals:* In 1996 in the Meru district of Kenya, twenty-five mother-daughter pairs took part in a six-day training session, during which they were told about the health effects of circumcision and coached on how to defend the decision not to be cut. The session culminated in a celebration in which the girls received gifts and "books of wisdom" prepared by their parents.

• *Employment for midwives:* In several African countries, programs have aimed at finding other ways for midwives and traditional healers to make a living. A soap factory set up near Umbada, Sudan, with help from Oxfam and UNICEF is one example.

• *Health education:* Many African governments have launched public-information campaigns. In Burkina Faso, for instance, a national committee has held awareness meetings and distributed teaching materials. A documentary film, *Ma fille ne sera pas excisée* ("My daughter will not be excised"), has been shown on national television. And in Sierra Leone, health workers found that when it was explained to women that genital surgery had caused their physical ailments, they were more willing to leave their daughters uncut.

So far the success of such pilot projects remains uncertain. The available statistics are disheartening: in Egypt, Eritrea and Mali the percentages of women circumcised remain the same among young and old. Attitudes, however, do seem to be shifting. In Eritrea men and women under twenty-five are much more likely than people in their forties to think the tradition should be abandoned. And in recent years in Burkina Faso, parents who are opposed to circumcision but who fear the wrath of aunts or grandmothers have been known to stage fake operations.

Genital Cutting in the West

Refugees and immigrants from Africa who arrive in Australia, Canada, Europe or the United States have brought genital mutilation more immediately to Western attention. On the basis of the 1990 U.S. Census, the Centers for Disease Control and Prevention in Atlanta, Georgia, has estimated that at least 168,000 girls and women in the United States have either been circumcised or are at risk. Between 1994 and 1998 the U.S. Congress and nine state governments have criminalized the practice, and similar laws have been passed in several European countries. So far in the United States, no one has been prosecuted under the new laws.

Meanwhile, Fauziya Kassindja, a twenty-year-old woman from Togo, spent more than a year behind bars, in detention centers and prisons in New Jersey and Pennsylvania, after fleeing to the United States in 1994 to avoid circumcision. Her mother, who remained in Togo, had sacrificed her inheritance and defied the family patriarch to help her escape. A U.S. immigration judge initially denied Kassindja's claim of persecution, saying her story lacked "rationality." Later, his ruling was overturned, and Kassindja was granted political asylum.

Western ignorance and incredulity regarding female circumcision have made life difficult and even dangerous for immigrant Africans. I recently met an infibulated Sudanese woman living in New England who was having trouble finding a gynecologist trained to treat her. "I am six months pregnant and I don't know what to expect," she told me fearfully. While pressing for an end to the practice, advocates must not ignore its victims. Perhaps exchange programs should be arranged for American gynecologists and obstetricians, to enable them to learn appropriate prenatal care from their African counterparts.

Too High a Price

Every society has rules to which its members are expected to conform. But for African women, belonging exacts too high a price. Whereas African men often have more than one wife and freely engage in extramarital sex, "the acceptable image of a woman with a place in society [is] that of one who is circumcised, docile, fertile, marriageable, hardworking, asexual and obedient," writes Olayinka Koso-Thomas, a Nigerian physician.

The irony is that, in a society that forces women to reconstruct their bodies in order to be socially and sexually acceptable, most men prefer sex with uncircumcised women. In a study of 300 Sudanese men, each of whom had one wife who had been infibulated and one or more who had not, 266 expressed a strong sexual preference for the uninfibulated wife. A second irony is that circumcision does not guarantee a woman a secure marriage; in fact, the opposite may be true. Infibulated women are more prone to fertility problems, which in Africa is grounds for being cast off by a husband. One study has shown that infibulated women in Sudan are more than twice as likely as other women to be divorced.

It might seem odd that women, not men, are the custodians of the ritual—in fact, a Sudanese man recently made headlines by filing a criminal lawsuit against his wife for having their two daughters circumcised while he was out of the country. Why do women subject their daughters to what they know firsthand to be a wrenchingly painful ordeal? Many are simply being practical. "I think that it is very important for the virginity of women to be protected if they want to get husbands who respect them," a fifty-five-year-old Sudanese mother of five girls told me. To get married and have children is a survival strategy in a society plagued by poverty, disease and illiteracy. The socioeconomic dependence of women on men colors their attitude toward circumcision.

But male oppression is not the biggest problem women face in Africa. Africans—men and women alike—must still cope with the ugly remnants of colonialism, the fact that they and their land have been exploited by Western nations and then abandoned. They are struggling to build democratic systems and economic stability from scratch. For African feminists, Western outrage about genital mutilation often seems misplaced. On a continent where millions of women do not have access to the basics of life—clean water, food, sanitation, education and health care—genital mutilation is not necessarily the top priority.

Studies have shown that the more educated women are, the less willing they are to have their daughters circumcised. I have no doubt that when African women have taken their rightful places in the various spheres of life, when they have gained social equality, political power, economic opportunities, and access to education and health care, genital mutilation will end. Women will make sure of that.

GENDER INEQUALITY AND POPULATION GROWTH

Amartya Sen

Population growth rates are rapidly falling in many parts of the world. However, as Amartya Sen writes, in some areas rates are falling very slowly, if at all. High rates of childbirth are often found in regions where women traditionally face gender inequity, he observes. Economic hardship, lack of access to family planning, and cultural and religious factors combine to compel many women to bear large numbers of children. However, Sen explains, programs that promote literacy, employment, and family planning for women appear to lead to a decline in birth rates. In addition, women's empowerment can sway religious and cultural beliefs that traditionally view women as fit only to be mothers and caretakers. By implementing gender equity, Sen assents, fertility rates can be reduced, which is good for women and the world. Sen is the master of Trinity College in Cambridge, England, and the author of *Development as Freedom*. He was awarded the Nobel Prize for economic science in 1998.

The magnitude of the population problem is frequently exaggerated. Anxious commentators have been terrifying others about imagined disasters for a very long time. That roaring tradition goes back at least 200 years, when Thomas Robert Malthus declared that the world was heavily overpopulated already and that the growth of food supply was losing the race with the growth of population. However, as in Malthus's time, food production now continues to grow significantly faster than world population, with the fastest expansion of food output per head occurring in relatively poor countries, such as China and India. What is particularly remarkable is that the rapid expansion of world food output has continued despite the reduced economic incentive to produce food, as a result of a sharp fall in food prices relative to other prices. Indeed, although international prices of wheat, rice and other staple foods, in constant US dollars, have fallen by more than 60 percent between 1950–52 and 1995–97, more and more of these crops are being produced, staying well ahead of population growth.

But there is a danger of complacency here. The fact that population growth is much slower than the growth of world output (of food as well as of industrial and other commodities) often generates undue placidity, reinforced by the further recognition (correct, as it happens) that fertility rates and population growth are coming down fast for the world as a whole and also for most regions of the world. This reassuring overall picture hides the fact that population growth rates are falling very fast in some regions and very slowly—sometimes not at all—in others.

It is, in fact, extremely important to avoid complacency in dealing with the population problem and to understand that it raises serious issues that are not particularly well captured by the old Malthusian perspective. One such issue is the environment—global as well as local. It is true that environmental adversities such as global warming are influenced by total consumption rather than the total size of the population (poor people consume much less and pollute far less). But one hopes that in the future the poorer nations of today will be rich as well, and the compound effect of a larger population and increased consumption could be devastating for the global environment. There is also the important challenge of overcrowding in a limited habitat. Children, too, have to be raised, not just food crops.

Frequent Childbearing Hurts Women

But perhaps the most immediate adversity caused by a high rate of population growth lies in the loss of freedom that women suffer when they are shackled by persistent bearing and rearing of children. Global warming is a distant effect compared with what population explosion does to the lives and well-being of mothers. Indeed, the most important—and perhaps the most neglected—aspect of the population debate is the adverse impact of high fertility imposed on women in societies where their voices don't count for much. Given the connection between over-frequent childbirth and the predicament of women, there are reasons to expect that an increase of gender equity, particularly in the decisional power of young women, would tend to lower fertility rates. Since women's interests are very badly served by high fertility rates imposed on them, they can be expected to correct this adversity if they have more power.

Why, then, do women have little decisional power in some societies, and how can that be remedied? There are various distinct influences to be considered here. First, social and economic handicaps (such as female illiteracy, lack of female employment opportunity and economic independence) contribute greatly to muffling women's voices in society and within the family. Second, the absence of knowledge or facilities of family planning can also be an important source of helplessness. Third, there are cultural, even religious, factors that place young women in a subservient position, making them accept the burden of constantly bearing and rearing children (as desired by the husband or the parents-in-law). These inequities may not even have to be physically enforced, since women's subservient role as well as frequent childbearing may appear "natural" when these practices have been sanctified by a long history that generates uncritical acceptance.

The Effect of Empowering Women

The promotion of female literacy, female employment opportunities and family-planning facilities, as well as open and informed public discussion of women's place in society, can enhance the voice and decisional role of women in family affairs and also bring about radical changes in the understanding of justice and injustice. Indeed, there is much evidence now, based on intercountry comparisons as well as interregional contrasts within a large country (such as recent empirical comparisons of the more than 300 districts that make up India), that women's empowerment (through employment, education, property rights, etc.) can have a very strong effect in reducing the fertility rate.

India is a statistician's paradise because of the tremendous variations among its distinct regions. While the total fertility rate for India as a whole is still substantially higher than the replacement level of two per couple, many districts in India not only have below-replacement fertility rates but also substantially lower fertility rates than, for example, the United States, Britain and China. The fertility rates have been falling more or less everywhere in India (the country average has fallen from six per couple some decades ago to about three per couple now), but the rate of decline has been extremely uneven. Speedy fertility declines in the states of Kerala, Tamil Nadu or Himachal Pradesh can be closely linked to the rapid enhancement of female education and other sources of empowerment of young women. Indeed, as a number of studies (by Mamta Murthi and Jean Dreze, among others) demonstrate, the two principal variables that explain the bulk of the interdistrict variations in fertility rates in India are female literacy and female employment opportunity. These achievements not only enhance women's voice in family decisions (thereby contributing directly to lowering fertility), they also have other favorable social effects. For example, female literacy has a strong impact in reducing child mortality rates, which also contributes, indirectly, to reducing fertility (since the desire to have a large family is often related to insuring support in one's old age from surviving progeny). The states in India with high fertility (for example, Uttar Pradesh, Bihar, Rajasthan) are precisely those that give few economic and educational opportunities to young women.

It is also interesting in this context to note that while China's sharp fertility decline is often attributed to coercive policies (like the "one-child family"), one could have expected a roughly similar decline because of China's excellent achievements in raising female education and employment. The contrast between China and India is a useful one to examine, in this context, since both countries—like many others in Asia—have had much gender-based inequality and persistent male preference in the treatment of children. As a whole, China has done far more than India to give women educational and economic opportunities. However, there are parts of India (which is much more diverse than China) that have done more than China in this respect. Kerala, for example—a sizable Indian state with about 30 million people—has a higher rate of female literacy than every province of China.

Kerala's rate of expansion of female literacy has also been faster than China's. Correspondingly, Kerala has experienced a substantially faster decline in fertility rates. While the Chinese fertility rate fell from 2.8 to 2.0 between 1979 (when the one-child policy was introduced) and 1991, it fell from 3 to 1.8 in the same period in Kerala. Kerala has kept its lead over China both in female education and in fertility decline (as of the year 2000, Kerala's fertility rate is around 1.7; China's, about 1.9). Also, thanks to the process of fertility decline being freely chosen without any coercion, the infant mortality rate has continued to fall fast in Kerala while it has not in China, even though they were roughly even in this respect in 1979. The female infant mortality rate now in China is, in fact, more than twice that in Kerala.

The Influence of Culture and Religion

Variations within India also bring out the important fact that even cultural and religious influences on fertility can themselves be swayed. For example, it has been argued that Muslim populations tend to have a higher fertility rate. Insofar as there is any truth to this, the linkage seems to operate mainly in an indirect way, through various correlates of gender inequality (including female illiteracy and lower employment opportunity). Significance is sometimes attached to the fact that Pakistan has a much higher fertility rate than India (around five, in contrast to three), but that divergence corresponds closely to the difference between the two countries in terms of female education, women's employment and other influences on women's empowerment.

Also, the Muslim population in India is itself very large—around 120 million—the third-largest among all countries in the world (despite the insistence of Hindu political activists as well as the Western press on describing multireligious and constitutionally secular India as a "mainly Hindu country"). As it happens, the most successful state in India in reducing fertility, Kerala, also has the highest percentage of Muslims among all the states, with the exception of Kashmir. In general, the fertility rates of Indian Muslims are much closer to those of other communities in the same region in India, including the Hindus, than to Muslims in Pakistan. Insofar as there are intercommunity contrasts in fertility within India, they too relate to such social and economic variables as education, employment and property rights, and altogether they are relatively minor within each state, in comparison with the large differences between the different Indian states—matching the contrasts in related social and economic variables.

It is also significant that Bangladesh, with a predominantly Muslim population, has had a sharp reduction in fertility rates, which can be associated with the gains that Bangladeshi women have recently made through the expansion of family-planning opportunities, greater involvement of women in economic activities (for example, through microcredit programs) and much public discussion and political activism on the need to change the prevailing pattern of gender disparity. In a mere decade and a half (between 1980 and 1996), Bangladesh's fertility rate has come down from 6.1 (close to Pakistan's today) to 3.4 (close to India's), and it is continuing to fall sharply. The bottom line, then, is this: While cultural and religious influences on fertility rates cannot be ignored, they are neither immutable nor independent of the social and economic factors through which the cultural connections work.

A Uniform Approach to Reducing Fertility

There are, of course, many different influences that operate on fertility rates, and it would be a mistake to look for one "magic variable" that would work uniformly well in reducing high fertility rates. What is needed instead is a unified approach that places different variables within a general framework of family decisions on fertility. The advantage of bringing gender equity and women's empowerment to the center of the stage is that they provide a broad perspective that can accommodate many of the major influences on fertility decisions. This includes acknowledging the role of educational development (including the schooling of girls), economic arrangements (including female job opportunities), social concerns (including the status of women) and cultural factors (including the value of equity in family decisions), as well as the more traditional variables that can assist family planning (such as the availability of family-planning facilities and access to medical attention). The expansion of family planning may appear to be just a demographic intervention, but the real opportunity to practice family planning can also be seen in the broader light of enhancing the decisional freedom of families in general and of vulnerable women in particular.

It is important to bring together, under a unified framework of understanding, the diverse influences on fertility reduction that have been identified in the empirical and statistical research. A variety of institutions have constructive roles in this crucial social transformation, including family-planning centers, elementary schools, land-reform facilities, microcredit organizations and free newspapers and other media for unrestrained public discussion. These distinct institutions have their respective roles, but there is a need to integrate the processes of social change that they separately but interactively induce. For example, the debates—often bitter—between advocates of family-planning facilities and female education must give way to a more integrated approach.

The crucial issue is the need to recognize that a responsible policy of fertility decline demands gender equity, which is, of course, crucially important for other reasons as well. The way forward is through more freedom and justice, not through more coercion and intimidation. The population problem is integrally linked with justice for women in particular. On this reasoning, it is also right to expect that advancing gender equity, through reversing the various social and economic handicaps that make women voiceless and powerless, may also be one of the best ways of saving the environment, working against global warming and countering the dangers of overcrowding and other adversities associated with population pressure. The voice of women is critically important for the world's future—not just for women's future.

THE INTERNATIONAL SEX TRADE

Leah Platt

Women from around the world often have to take jobs in what is known as the informal economy in order to support themselves. In many cases, writes Leah Platt, these jobs are in the sex industry, whether the women live in the developing world or are migrants to developed nations. She finds that prostitutes are subject to the same poor working conditions and exploitation as female workers in other informal economies, such as sweatshops. However, Platt reveals, labor laws designed to protect women in informal economies often do not apply to sex work because of the moral aspects of the job. Sex work deserves the same labor law protection as any other job, she argues. Platt believes that addressing the economic realities of sex work, instead of focusing on the moral aspects, will lead to effective policies for change. Platt is a writing fellow with the *American Prospect*, a magazine that looks at current issues from a liberal perspective.

On the night of September 10, 1997, Toronto police officers raided more than a dozen apartments suspected of being houses of ill repute. Twenty-two women, including the alleged madam, Wai Hing "Kitty" Chu, were charged on a total of 750 prostitution and immigration-related charges. All of the women were Asian and spoke no more than a few words of English.

The press accounts of the raid were by turns titillating and full of moral outrage. According to the *San Jose Mercury News*, the women were helpless victims, "pretty, naive country bumpkins" who were exploited by an international crime syndicate (the U.S. police collaborated on parallel raids in San Jose). In a piece for *The Toronto Sun*, with the lurid headline "Sex Slaves: Fodder for Flesh Factories," a reporter profiled "Mary," a Thai prostitute, who obligingly described her first trick, a fumbling failure made to sound almost endearing.

It is a familiar story by now: poor, vulnerable women from Thailand or the Ukraine promised jobs as nannies or models in Western cities, only to find themselves pressed into service as prostitutes to pay off travel debts and line the pockets of their traffickers. As long as

Excerpted from "Regulating the Global Brothel," by Leah Platt, *American Prospect*, July 2–July 16, 2001. Copyright © 2001 by the *American Prospect*. Reprinted with permission.

the women were portrayed as misled innocents, it was easy for Toronto readers to sympathize.

But readers' pity quickly turned to anger when it was revealed, a few days later, that most of the women had known exactly what kind of work they had been recruited to do. As the *Toronto Star* summed up a few months later, "public opinion did an instant about-face" when police revealed that the women "had willingly come to Canada to ply their trade; wiretaps caught them boasting, long distance, about the money they were earning." Now, the women were considered "hardened delinquents, illegal immigrants, tawdry, dismissible, selling their bodies of their own free will."

Nothing became of the initial allegations of labor abuses. There had been rumors of debt bondage, a form of indentured servitude that requires migrants to finance their travel expenses (which are frequently inflated) by working without pay; of confinement; of shifts that lasted 18 hours. But before these charges could be investigated, the women were released on their own recognizance and disappeared from view, dismissed by the media as common whores.

Sex Work Is a Form of Labor

What is it that separates a Thai woman turning tricks in a cramped Toronto apartment from a Mexican immigrant toiling in a sweatshop in the suburbs of Los Angeles? Why does the former draw our scorn, the latter our sympathy? Clearly, many people react uncomfortably to the idea of sex as just another good that may be purchased on the open market. Yet for the women who make their living as strippers, escorts, prostitutes, and porn stars, sexual activity at the workplace is a job—a repetitive task that can be as unerotic and downright boring as cutting pork shoulders on an assembly line or sewing sneakers in a Nike factory. As such, doesn't sex work deserve the full protection of U.S. labor laws?

One reason that sex work doesn't currently benefit from such labor protections in the United States is that the feminist community, which is the champion of women's rights in the workplace in many realms, remains bitterly divided over prostitution. On one side are the abolitionists, who call prostitution a crime against women, akin to rape or domestic abuse; on the other side are the pro-choicers, for whom the rhetoric of victimization is itself demeaning, and who say that women should be able to do whatever they want with their own bodies, including renting them out for pay.

The two sides talk past each other, particularly at the extremes. Prostitutes, the controversial firebrand Camille Paglia has said, are "very competent, very professional. They look fabulous! I've always felt that prostitutes are in control of the streets, not victims. I admire that—zooming here and there, escaping the police, being shrewd, living by your wits, being street smart." To Donna Hughes, on the other hand, the director of the women's studies program at the University of Rhode Island, the idea of selling a sex act like a trip through the car wash is inherently degrading, and in practice is often accompanied by rape, intimidation, and cruelty. "A lot of people don't know what prostitution is," she told me angrily. "They don't know what it really takes to have sex with five strangers a day. What most people know about prostitution is based on myths and misinformation."

But while feminists debate the "sex" part of sex work—is it degrading or liberating?—they generally ignore the "work" part. Neither Paglia's paean to the hooker-as-rugged-individualist nor Hughes's lament for the little-girl-lost captures the often mundane reality of illicit prostitution: It is a job without overtime pay, health insurance, or sick leave—and usually without recourse against the abuses of one's employer, which can include being required to have sex without a condom and being forced to turn tricks in order to work off crushing debts. Given that the sex industry exists and probably always will (they don't call it the oldest profession for nothing), what should be done about its exploitative conditions?

Sex Work Goes Global

That question was vexing enough when prostitution was primarily a local issue. But sex work is an increasingly global service. In the language of international trade, sexual services are commonly "imported" into places like the United States from the developing world. Men from wealthy countries frequent the semi-regulated sex sectors in Cuba, the Dominican Republic, and Thailand—a phenomenon known as "sex tourism." And women from countries in Southeast Asia, Africa, and eastern Europe migrate to the industrialized world to work in the domestic sex industries. The United Nations estimates annual profits from the trade in sex workers like the Thai women arrested in Canada to be $7 billion.

While there are no precise statistics on the number of women who enter the United States from abroad to work as prostitutes—either voluntarily as immigrants or involuntarily as victims of trafficking—a recent report by the Central Intelligence Agency (CIA) estimates that roughly 50,000 women and children are brought into the country by traffickers each year. (This figure includes trafficking victims who work in brothels as well as those who work in sweatshops and as domestic servants.)

The crime of trafficking in women has attracted a great deal of attention from policy makers in Congress and the international community. The European Commission highlighted action against the "modern day slave trade" as part of its commemoration of International Women's Day in March 2001. The UN Convention Against Transnational Organized Crime, which was signed in December 2000, included a separate protocol on the prevention of trafficking in

women and children. Here at home, Congress passed the Victims of
Trafficking and Violence Prevention Act in a nearly unanimous vote
in October 2000, a move that President Bill Clinton hailed as "the
most significant step we've ever taken to secure the health and safety
of women at home and around the world." Minnesota's liberal Senator Paul Wellstone, one of the bill's co-sponsors, said that "something
important is in the air when such a broad coalition of people—including Bill Bennett, Gloria Steinem, Rabbi David Sapperstein, Ann Jordan, and Chuck Colson—work together for the passage of legislation." And what's not to love about a bill that can be dressed up
alternatively as a victory for women's rights, a way to get tough on
crime, and a curb on immigration? As Ann Jordan of the International Human Rights Law Group puts it, "there is no way that any
politician could say he is opposed to this bill. It was a win-win bill for
everyone." Even the Christian right was satisfied; Jordan explains that
"evangelicals took on trafficking as one of their big projects" in order
to rescue innocent women from the sin of prostitution.

Trafficking and Smuggling

But in all this self-congratulatory rhetoric about protecting innocent
girls, some of the harder questions never got asked. What is the distinction between "trafficking," say, and alien smuggling, or between
trafficking and labor exploitation? According to the CIA report, trafficking "usually involves long-term exploitation for economic gain,"
whereas alien smuggling is a limited exchange—an illegal immigrant
pays a smuggler to be transported or escorted across the border and
there the economic relationship ends.

But in practice the two crimes blend together: Hopeful migrants
often can't afford the price of their passage and arrive in the country
in debt to their smuggler; the smuggler in effect becomes a trafficker.
As migrants try to pay off their loans, they are often caught in abusive
situations, forced to work long hours in unsafe and unsanitary conditions. The most notorious example of this mistreatment is the El
Monte case, named for a town in Southern California where 72 Thai
migrants were found in 1995 held against their will in a warren of
apartments that doubled as a garment factory. To pay off their travel
debts, the migrants were stripped of their passports and forced to
work at sewing machines for more than 80 hours a week at a negligi-
ble wage, surrounded by barbed wire. After the operation was raided
by federal and state agents, the perpetrators pleaded guilty to indentured servitude in order to avoid more severe kidnapping charges and
were sentenced to between two and seven years in prison.

The facts of the El Monte case parallel the alleged misdeeds in the
Toronto brothel: The perpetrator helped immigrants enter the country illegally and the immigrants were forced (either through violence
or because of mounting debts) to work in substandard conditions for

below-minimum wages. But addressing Toronto-type situations with specific legislation like the Victims of Trafficking and Violence Prevention Act implies that foreign women working in the sex industry are different in kind from foreign laborers in other exploitative industries. There is arguably something to this implication; sex workers are more susceptible to rape and other forms of violent degradation. Yet legislation like the Victims of Trafficking and Violence Prevention Act implicitly seems to exempt sex workers (and their exploiters) from the labor laws that already exist to protect them—making them instead subject to the specific crime of "sex trafficking." Such laws obscure the fact that for the most part the abuses that afflict prostitutes are the sort that can befall all migrant workers.

Existing Laws Should Protect Prostitutes

"Prostitutes," writes Jo Bindman of Anti-Slavery International, "are subjected to abuses which are similar in nature to those experienced by others working in low-status jobs in the informal sector." In her 1997 report, "Redefining Prostitution as Sex Work on the International Agenda," Bindman argues that mistreatment of prostitutes—everything from arbitrary arrest and police brutality to pressure to perform certain sexual acts at work—should not be thought of as hazards of the trade or as conditions that loose women bring upon themselves but as abuses of human rights and labor standards.

In other words, rather than design new legislation to combat the crimes of "sexual slavery" or "trafficking in women," we should prosecute alien smuggling, trafficking, debt bondage, and labor exploitation under existing national and international codes. The International Labor Organization (ILO) has signed conventions on forced labor (1930), holidays with pay (1936), the protection of the right to organize (1948), the protection of wages (1949), and migration for employment (1949), but because of our intuitive sense that sex work should be marginalized as immoral and degrading to women, none of these rules has been applied to the gray market in sexual services. Our well-meaning desire to "protect" women forces the prostitution industry underground and out of the reach of established labor statutes.

Why Prostitutes Migrate

As hard as life can be for prostitutes who lack formal labor protections, it is often still harder for migrant prostitutes, who as both illegal immigrants and participants in an illegal industry are doubly marginalized. The Network of Sex Work Projects, an informal alliance of human rights organizations, warns that the dual "illegality of sex work and migration" allows smugglers and brothel owners to "exert an undue amount of power and control" over foreign sex workers. Employers threaten migrant sex workers with deportation if they inform the authorities about inhumane labor practices—and even if women could report their situation, the authorities might not take it seriously.

The migration of sex workers to the developed world is part of a wider pattern that sociologists call the "feminization" of migration. Until very recently, most labor migrants were men who worked in mining, manufacturing, and construction. If women migrated, they did so under family reunification statutes, often with children in tow. As industrialized economies become more service oriented, the jobs available to migrants are increasingly in the "female" sector, which includes everything from maids to nannies to exotic dancers. "The latest figures from the ILO indicate that more than 50 percent of labor migrants are women," says Marian Wijers, a fellow at the Netherlands' Clara Wichmann Center for Women and Law in Utrecht. "But the economic situation is different now than it was for men a generation ago. Male migrants entered the formal labor market through formal channels. They didn't have the most attractive types of employment," she notes, "but at least they had work permits. Women have been relegated to the informal sector in traditional women's work: domestic and sexual services, either in the sex industry or in arranged marriages. These jobs are often not recognized as 'work'; there are no labor protections for them, no access to legal working permits."

Not All Sex Workers Are Victims

Despite the very real conditions of abuse, Wijers is careful not to call all low-paid female immigrants—or all migrant prostitutes—victims. For many women now, as has been the case for men for centuries, migration is a calculated financial decision, with prostitution seen as a way to make money. Sex work, like providing paid domestic services and child care, is a way to support family or children back home or to start a new life in the West. "These women made a conscious decision to improve their situation through migration," Wijers explains. "It is possible that they expected another job—and of course, no one expects to be held in slavery-like conditions. But these women are intelligent, enterprising, and courageous. It is quite a step to leave your family and your security to go abroad, into a situation where you don't know exactly what to expect."

Wijers has staked out a defensible middle ground between the strict abolitionists and the prostitution-as-self-expression promoters: She supports a woman's right to control over her own body, as well as a prostitute's volition as an economic actor, without valorizing sex work as a liberating profession. As one of the chief investigators for a report on trafficking prepared for the UN Special Rapporteur on Violence Against Women, Wijers is one of the world's foremost experts on forced prostitution, but she finds the narrative of victimization supported by the United Nations to be sentimental and overly simplistic. The reality in her native country, the Netherlands, is more nuanced. "Some of the first women to come from abroad were from the Dominican Republic and Colombia," she says. "They were clearly disadvantaged, recruited in cruel ways, forced into terrible conditions—all the cliches. But when you have spent some period of time in a country, you start to make contacts and to organize. Soon these women were sending for their aunt or their sister—they were organizing the migration of female friends and relatives. Within a few 'generations' of migration, this group of women learned Dutch and became more independent."

One of the most reliable studies of sex tourism, conducted by the ILO in 1998, corroborates Wijers's observations. Based on interviews with thousands of sex workers in Indonesia, Malaysia, the Philippines, and Thailand, the report concluded that "while many current studies highlight the tragic stories of individual prostitutes, especially of women and children deceived or coerced into the practice, many workers entered for pragmatic reasons and with a general sense of awareness of the choice they were making." Almost all of the women surveyed said they knew what kind of work they would be doing before they began; half, in fact, responded that they found their job on a friend's recommendation.

The Benefits of Legalization

In order to use labor laws to protect women in the sex industry, the legal status of prostitution and its offshoots—brothel keeping, pimping, soliciting, paying for sex—would need to be re-examined. After all, the Department of Justice does not ensure minimum wages for drug runners or concern itself with working conditions in the Mob. But whether or not we approve of sex work or would want our daughters to be thus employed, the moral argument for condemnation starts to fall apart when we consider the conditions of abuse suffered by real women working in the industry. Criminalization has been as unsuccessful in dismantling the sex industry as it has been in eliminating the drug trade and preventing back-alley abortions. Sex work is here to stay, and by recognizing it as paid labor governments can guarantee fair treatment as well as safe and healthy work environments—including overtime and vacation pay, control over condom use, and the fight to collective bargaining.

A decision to re-evaluate the legal status of the sex industry in the United States would not be without international precedent. Prostitution is legal (while subject to varying degrees of regulation) in England, France, and many other parts of Europe. In 1999, Germany eliminated the legal definition of prostitution as an "immoral trade," thus allowing sex workers to participate in the national health insurance plan. Prostitution is also legal in parts of South America and the Caribbean, and in some counties in Nevada. Prostitutes' unions have sprung up in Cambodia, Hong Kong, India, and Mexico, and groups like COYOTE (Call Off Your Old Tired Ethics) advocate for sex workers' rights in the United States.

In areas where prostitution is legal, brothel keeping—or profiting from the proceeds of prostitution—remains a crime. Even the Netherlands, a country notorious for its laissez-faire attitude toward sex work, legalized brothels only in 1999; and the concern that, as sanctioned businesses, brothels would sprout up on every street corner there has proved unfounded. Brothels are now subject to the same building codes and municipal ordinances as any other business—including zoning laws that keep brothels contained in established red-light districts.

Legalization in the Netherlands

As one of the only countries with a fully decriminalized sex industry, the Netherlands provides the fullest illustration of how legalization can operate. Amsterdam's red-light district occupies a maze of narrow streets in the oldest part of the city. Residents who have no interest in frequenting the sex shops can avoid the area without inconvenience. Inside the district, which is marked off with strings of red lights, prostitutes sit in storefront windows to display their wares (100 guilders, or roughly $50, for a 15-minute "suck and fuck"), alongside topless bars porn and sex toy shops, and the neon lights of peep show emporiums. Even in the dead of winter, packs of foreign men gather in the narrow alleys to gawk and knock on windows. Some of the women behind the windows look Dutch, but Marisha Majoor, who greeted me at the Prostitution Information Center's storefront, corrects this impression. "Most of the blond girls are from other European Union countries, like Sweden and Germany," she says. Dutch women, who can work in the comfort of their own homes, don't bother with the hustle of the red-light neighborhood.

Until 1999, Amsterdam's windows were full of illegal immigrants from Africa and eastern Europe. Brothel and club owners estimated that between 40 percent and 75 percent of the women in the red-light district were working illegally. All of that changed with the legalization of brothels. "Of course," says Marieke van Doorninck, a research fellow at the Mr. A. de Graaf Stichting Institute for Prostitution Issues in Amsterdam, "brothel owners were technically never allowed to work with illegal migrants, but the practice was condoned for years. If an illegal worker was discovered, all that could happen is that she would be deported and the club owner would be given a fine. There was no real incentive for the brothel owners to deny jobs to illegal migrants. Now they can lose their license."

There are still a few African women working in the red-light district. Some of them have married Dutch men; others have forged passports from Italy or Greece, allowing them to work in the European Union. One landlord, a gray-haired, heavyset man known as

Marcel, owns 20 windows; his "tenants" are mostly from Africa. He claims that all of his "girls" have legitimate papers and, when pressed, pulls out a blue binder stuffed with photocopied passports from Ghana and Nigeria.

The passports may very well be real, but according to van Doorninck, the working papers could not have been. "In other lines of work," she explains, "if a boss can show that there is no person from the EU that can do the job, then he can hire someone from outside." Farmers, for example, regularly request allowances for agricultural workers. "But the sex industry is shut out from this regulation. There is no legal way for a woman from outside the EU to work in prostitution." Sex workers are also specifically excluded from the immigration regulations governing the self-employed. Potential immigrants from outside the European Union "can apply for working papers if they show a viable business plan and can prove that they are capable of taking care of themselves without becoming dependent on the state," says van Doornick. "But foreigners who apply to settle in the Netherlands as self-employed prostitutes are in principle rejected on the grounds that their activities do not serve the country's interests."

Illegal Migrants and Prostitution

The women working in Marcel's windows are lucky. Most of the Asian, African, and eastern-European women left in Amsterdam are working on the street or in unregulated black-market brothels. "By making it more difficult for foreign women to work in legal places, where they have been condoned for ages, they are forced to leave or to work in an illegal setting," van Doorninck points out. "In a way, the government stimulates trafficking by leaving no options for the women who are already here."

The Dutch government's decision to regulate brothels was based less on morality than on economics. The sex sector had long been "officially tolerated" (or in Dutch, *gedoogt*); by legalizing its activities, the government is able to collect revenues from licenses and tax. And from the workers' perspective, legalizing the sex industry—and thus barring foreign women from working in licensed brothels—follows from a classic trade-protectionist motive. Why offer jobs to non-Europeans when there are plenty of women in Holland and elsewhere in the European Union who are willing to work in the Dutch sex industry?

Before the change in brothels' status, "there was definitely tension between Dutch prostitutes and the migrant workers, a competition over prices," remembers Wijers. "Because the illegal women had no documents, they were willing to work for less and Dutch women started to feel uneasy." Foreign women "spoil the market," the Prostitution Information Center's Majoor told a team of American and Dutch college students researching the condition of illegal prostitutes in 2000. It makes you furious when some guy keeps knocking at your door, saying, 'Okay, but a little way down the street, they are only asking 25 guilders." Majoor, like most of the Dutch women who work in the sex industry, belongs to the Red Thread, a lobbying group akin to a union. The Red Thread does not allow illegal migrants to join. "When a hotel like the Hilton suddenly brings in an Hungarian pianist who is willing to work for less money, longer hours, without social insurance, Dutch pianists will complain," Wijers notes. "It is the same mechanism in the sex industry as in other labor sectors."

Improving Conditions in the Sex Industry

The Dutch experience with decriminalization suggests that the reaction of the sex industry to the stresses of globalization is not unlike that of, say, the garment industry here in the United States. Domestic workers resent immigrants, who are eager to find work at any pay and consequently create downward pressure on wages. Arriving in the country with few resources and little command of the language, immigrants are often shunted into the informal economy, which in this case means shady makeshift brothels and back-of-the-bus-station encounters.

Legalization may be limited in what it can do to reach the nearly invisible population of illegal migrants who work internationally in the sex industry. But that's also true of the Victims of Trafficking and Violence Prevention Act and the protocol included in the UN Convention Against Transnational Organized Crime. Both of the latter measures define trafficking as an explicitly sexual crime—an act of violence against women—rather than as a by-product of an ever more global marketplace and the increasing feminization of migration. Any policy that will truly improve the often deplorable working conditions in the international sex industry must confront the economic realities of the profession without getting distracted by the sexual ones.

To those who feel their moral hackles rising at the prospect, Ann Jordan of the International Human Rights Law Group presents a compelling analogy: "We don't support a woman's right to choose because we think abortion is a great thing," she says, "but because we believe fundamentally that women should have control over their own reproductive capacity. The same argument can be made for prostitution. Women who decide for whatever reason to sell sex should have the right to control their own body"—and should be assured of basic protection on the job. As with abortions, we can dream of a day when sex work is safe, legal, and rare.

ORGANIZATIONS TO CONTACT

The editors have compiled the following list of organizations concerned with the issues presented in this book. The descriptions are derived from materials provided by the organizations. All have publications or information available for interested readers. The list was compiled on the date of publication of the present volume; the information provided here may change. Be aware that many organizations take several weeks or longer to respond to inquiries, so allow as much time as possible.

American Civil Liberties Union (ACLU)
125 Broad St., 18th Fl., New York, NY 10004-2400
(212) 549-2500 • to order publications: (800) 775-2258 • fax: (212) 549-2646
e-mail: aclu@aclu.org • website: www.aclu.org

The ACLU is dedicated to defending Americans' civil rights as guaranteed by the U.S. Constitution. It works to establish equality before the law, regardless of race, color, sexual orientation, gender, or national origin. The ACLU publishes and distributes policy statements, pamphlets, and reports, including the *Women's Rights Project Annual Report* and the periodic newsletter *Civil Liberties Alert.*

Amnesty International (AI)
322 8th Ave., New York, NY 10001
(212) 807-8400 • fax: (212) 627-1451
e-mail: admin-us@aiusa.org • website: www.amnesty.org

This grassroots activist organization works to protect and preserve human rights worldwide. AI is dedicated to the release of all prisoners of conscience, fair and prompt trials for political prisoners, and the abolishment of torture, executions, and other violations of human rights. The group supports U.S. ratification of the United Nations Convention on the Elimination of All Forms of Discrimination Against Women and participates in the campaign to eradicate female genital mutilation. Its publications include the quarterly newsletter *Amnesty Action*, the annual *Amnesty International Report*, and various briefing papers and special reports.

Eagle Forum
PO Box 618, Alton, IL 62002
(618) 462-5415 • fax: (618) 462-8909
e-mail: eagle@eagleforum.org • website: www.eagleforum.org

The Eagle Forum is dedicated to preserving traditional family values. It promotes the belief that mothers should stay at home with their children, and it endorses policies that support the traditional family and reduce government intervention in family issues. The forum opposes feminism, arguing that the movement has harmed women and families. The organization publishes the monthly *Phyllis Schlafly Report.*

The Heritage Foundation
214 Massachusetts Ave. NE, Washington, DC 20002-4999
(202) 546-4400 • fax: (202) 546-8328
e-mail: info@heritage.org • website: www.heritage.org

The Heritage Foundation is a conservative public policy research institute that advocates limited government, free-market principles, and individual liberty. It opposes affirmative action for women and minorities and believes the private sector, not government, should be relied upon to ease social problems and improve the status of women. The foundation publishes the bimonthly journal *Policy Review* as well as hundreds of monographs, books, and papers on public policy issues.

Independent Women's Forum (IWF)
PO Box 3058, Arlington, VA 22203-0058
(703) 558-4991 • (800) 224-6000 • fax: (703) 558-4994
e-mail: info@iwf.org • website: www.iwf.org

The forum affirms the family as the foundation of society and advocates policies that promote individual responsibility and limited government. The IWF works to foster public education and debate about legal, social, and economic policies affecting women and families. Its publications include the *Women's Quarterly*, the quarterly newsletter *Ex Femina*, policy statements, press releases, surveys, and special reports, such as "Lying in a Room of One's Own: How Women's Studies Miseducates Students" and "Women, Work, and Family: Achieving a Balance."

International Labor Organization (ILO)
Washington Branch Office
1828 L St. NW, #600, Washington, DC 20036
(202) 653-7652 • fax: (202) 653-7687
e-mail: ilo@ilo.org • website: www.ilo.org

A specialized agency of the United Nations, the ILO works to promote basic human rights through improved working and living conditions by enhancing opportunities for those who are excluded from meaningful salaried employment. The ILO pioneered such landmarks of industrial society as the eight-hour workday, maternity protection, and workplace safety regulations. It offers a variety of material, including policy statements, reports, training manuals, CD-ROMs, the videotape *Her Way to Work: The Road to Quality Jobs for Women*, and the books *Gender and Jobs: Sex Segregation of Occupations in the World* and *The Sex Sector: The Economic and Social Bases of Prostitution in Southeast Asia*.

National Committee on Pay Equity (NCPE)
PO Box 34446, Washington, DC 20043-4446
(301) 277-1033 • fax: (301) 277-4451
e-mail: fairpay@patriot.net • website: www.feminist.com/fairpay

NCPE is a national coalition of labor, women's, and civil rights organizations and individuals working to achieve pay equity by eliminating sex- and race-based wage discrimination. Its publications include the *News from NCPE* newsletter and numerous books and briefing papers on the issue of pay equity.

National Council of Women's Organizations (NCWO)
733 15th St. NW, Suite 1011, Washington, DC 20005
(202) 393-7122 • fax: (202) 387-7915
e-mail: info@womensorganizations.org
website: www.womensorganizations.org

The NCWO is a nonpartisan network of more than one hundred organizations, including grassroots, research, service, media, and legal advocacy groups. NCWO's member organizations work together to address women's issues, including equal employment opportunity, economic equity, media equality, education, job training, welfare reform, and women's health and reproductive rights. The council publishes the electronic newsletter *NCWO Alert-Action Bulletin*.

National Organization for Women (NOW)
733 15th St. NW, 2nd Fl., Washington, DC 20005
(202) 628-8669 • fax: (202) 785-8576
e-mail: now@now.org • website: www.now.org

NOW is one of the largest and most influential feminist organizations in the United States. Through education and litigation, it supports equal rights for women in all areas of life, equal pay for women workers, the right to safe legal abortion and birth control, and the elimination of violence against women. NOW advocates equality for military servicewomen and favors allowing women to serve in combat roles. The organization publishes the *National NOW Times*, policy statements, articles, and news releases.

National Right to Life Committee (NRLC)
512 10th St. NW, Washington, DC 20004
(202) 626-8800
e-mail: nrlc@nrlc.org • website: www.nrlc.org

NRLC opposes abortion and advocates alternatives such as adoption. The committee's ultimate goal is to protect unborn children through the passage of legislation banning abortion. It encourages ratification of a constitutional amendment granting embryos and fetuses the same right to life as children and adults. NRLC publishes the brochure *When Does Life Begin?* and the monthly newspaper *National Right to Life News*.

National Women's Law Center (NWLC)
11 Dupont Circle NW, Suite 800, Washington, DC 20036
(202) 588-5180 • fax: (202) 588-5185
e-mail: info@nwlc.org • website: www.nwlc.org

The NWLC was formed in 1972 to work for the advancement of women and girls in all aspects of their lives. The center brings women's issues to the attention of policy makers, researchers, and the public, focusing on education, employment opportunities, economic status, child care, and women's health and reproductive rights. NWLC's publications include the report "The Supreme Court and Women's Rights: Fundamental Protections Hang in the Balance," the booklet *Take Action: Get Your Prescription Contraceptives Covered—A Practical Guide for Employees*, and the quarterly newsletter *NWLC Update*.

9to5 National Association of Working Women
1430 W. Peachtree St., # 610, Atlanta, GA 30309
(414) 274-0925 • (800) 522-0925
e-mail: naww9to5@execpc.com • website: www.9to5.org

The association is the leading membership organization for working women. It utilizes class-action lawsuits and public information campaigns to achieve change on issues including discrimination against pregnant women, sexual harassment in the workplace, and pay equity. It publishes books, reports, videotapes, lesson plans, the annual fact sheet "9to5 Profile of Working Women," and the bimonthly newsletter *9to5 Newsline*.

Planned Parenthood Federation of America (PPFA)
810 Seventh Ave., New York, NY 10019
(212) 541-7800 • fax: (212) 245-1845
e-mail: communications@ppfa.org • website: www.plannedparenthood.org

PPFA works to ensure the right of individuals to make their own reproductive decisions without governmental interference. The federation promotes research and the advancement of technology in reproductive health care. It also provides contraception, abortion, and family planning services at clinics located throughout the United States. Among its extensive publications are the pamphlet *Choosing Abortion: Questions and Answers*, the fact sheet "Unsafe Abortion Around the World," and the article "The Link Between Gender-Based Violence and Sexual and Reproductive Health."

United Nations Development Fund for Women (UNIFEM)
304 E. 45th St., 15th Fl., New York, NY 10017
(212) 906-6400 • fax (212) 906-6705
e-mail: unifem@undp.org • website: www.unifem.undp.org

The United Nations Development Fund for Women provides direct support for women's projects and promotes the inclusion of women in the decision-making process of development programs throughout the world. UNIFEM provides these services through its various chapters, namely, UNIFEM in Africa, UNIFEM in Asia and the Pacific, UNIFEM in Latin America and the Caribbean, and UNIFEM at the Global Level. It publishes the monthly newsletters *UNIFEM News* and the *Canadian Committee News* and the electronic news bulletin *UNIFEM Currents*.

U.S. Equal Employment Opportunity Commission (EEOC)
1801 L St. NW, Washington, DC 20507
(202) 663-4900 • (800) 669-4000
website: www.eeoc.gov

The mission of the EEOC is to promote equal opportunity in employment through administrative and judicial enforcement of the federal civil rights laws and through education and technical assistance. It publishes numerous reports, fact sheets, and press releases pertaining to affirmative action, sexual harassment, and discrimination in the workplace.

Wellesley Centers for Women (WCW)
Wellesley College, 106 Central St., Wellesley, MA 02481
(781) 283-2500 • fax: (781) 283-2504
e-mail: wcw@wellesley.edu • website: www.wcwonline.org

The WCW unites the Center for Research on Women and the Stone Center for Developmental Services and Studies in an interdisciplinary community of scholars engaged in research, training, analysis, and action. The WCW focuses its investigations on critical areas in the lives of women and girls, including such topics as domestic violence, sexual harassment, balancing work and family, and mental health. Information gathered by the WCW is provided to individuals and institutions in an effort to promote policies and practices that benefit women. WCW publishes the *Research Report* twice a year, as well as numerous studies and reports.

Wider Opportunities for Women (WOW)
1001 Connecticut Ave. NW, Suite 930, Washington, DC 20036
(202) 464-1596 • fax: (202) 464-1660
e-mail: info@wowonline.org • website: www.wowonline.org

WOW seeks to expand employment opportunities for women by overcoming sex-stereotypic education and training, work segregation, and discrimination in employment practices and wages. The organization sponsors programs that emphasize literacy and technical skills, welfare-to-work transition, career development, and women's access to high-wage nontraditional occupations. In addition to pamphlets and fact sheets, WOW publishes the quarterly newsletter *Women at Work*.

BIBLIOGRAPHY

Books

Marjorie Agosin, ed.
Women, Gender, and Human Rights: A Global Perspective. New Brunswick, NJ: Rutgers University Press, 2001.

Rosalyn Baxandall and Linda Gordon, eds.
Dear Sisters: Dispatches from the Women's Liberation Movement. New York: Basic Books, 2000.

Kathleen C. Berkeley
The Women's Liberation Movement in America. Westport, CT: Greenwood, 1999.

Rosemary Crompton, ed.
Restructuring Gender Relations and Employment: The Decline of the Male Breadwinner. New York: Oxford University Press, 1999.

Clare Cushman, ed.
Supreme Court Decisions and Women's Rights: Milestones to Equality. Washington, DC: CQ Press, 2001.

Parvin Darabi and Romin P. Thomson
Rage Against the Veil: The Courageous Life and Death of an Islamic Dissident. Amherst, NY: Prometheus Books, 1999.

Anne Dickson
Women at Work: Strategies for Survival and Success. London: Kogan Page, 2000.

Ellen Carol DuBois
Feminism and Suffrage: The Emergence of an Independent Women's Movement in America, 1848–1869. Ithaca, NY: Cornell University Press, 1999.

Betty Friedan
The Feminine Mystique. New York: W.W. Norton, 2001.

Diana Furchtgott-Roth and Christine Stolba
The Feminist Dilemma: When Success Is Not Enough. Washington, DC: AEI Press, 2001.

Germaine Greer
The Whole Woman. New York: Anchor Books, 2000.

International Labour Office
ABC of Women Workers' Rights and Gender Equality. Geneva, Switzerland: International Labour Office, 2000.

Robert Max Jackson
Destined for Equality: The Inevitable Rise of Women's Status. Cambridge, MA: Harvard University Press, 1998.

Fay Afaf Kanafani
Nadia, Captive of Hope: Memoir of an Arab Woman. Armonk, NY: M.E. Sharpe, 1998.

Eva Feder Kittay
Love's Labor: Essays on Women, Equality, and Dependency. New York: Routledge, 1999.

Jill Liddington and Jill Norris
One Hand Tied Behind Us: The Rise of the Women's Suffrage Movement. New York: New York University Press, 2000.

Martha Fetherolf Loutfi, ed.
Women, Gender and Work: What Is Equality and How Do We Get There? Geneva, Switzerland: International Labour Office, 2001.

151

John F. McClymer — *This High and Holy Moment: The First National Woman's Rights Convention, Worcester, 1850.* Fort Worth, TX: Harcourt Brace College, 1999.

Karen Messing — *One-Eyed Science: Occupational Health and Women Workers.* Philadelphia: Temple University Press, 1998.

Rosalind P. Petchesky and Karen Judd, eds. — *Negotiating Reproductive Rights: Women's Perspectives Across Countries and Cultures.* New York: Zed Books, 1998.

William Petrocelli and Barbara Kate Repa — *Sexual Harassment on the Job: What It Is and How to Stop It.* Berkeley, CA: Nolo Press, 1998.

Anika Rahman and Nahid Toubia, eds. — *Female Genital Mutilation: A Guide to Laws and Policies Worldwide.* New York: Zed Books, 2000.

Aruna Rao, Rieky Stuart, and David Kelleher — *Gender at Work: Organizational Change for Equality.* West Hartford, CT: Kumarian Press, 1999.

Rachel Roth — *Making Women Pay: The Hidden Costs of Fetal Rights.* Ithaca, NY: Cornell University Press, 2000.

Diana E.H. Russell and Roberta A. Harmes, eds. — *Femicide in Global Perspective.* New York: Teachers College Press, 2001.

Rickie Solinger, ed. — *Abortion Wars: A Half Century of Struggle, 1950–2000.* Berkeley: University of California Press, 1998.

Lynn Walter, ed. — *Women's Rights: A Global View.* Westport, CT: Greenwood, 2001.

Geoffrey C. Ward — *Not for Ourselves Alone: The Story of Elizabeth Cady Stanton and Susan B. Anthony.* New York: Knopf, 1999.

Carol S. Weisman — *Women's Health Care: Activist Traditions and Institutional Change.* Baltimore, MD: Johns Hopkins University Press, 1998.

Christa Wichterich — *The Globalized Woman: Reports from a Future of Inequality.* New York: Zed Books, 2000.

Linda Wirth — *Breaking Through the Glass Ceiling: Women in Management.* Geneva, Switzerland: International Labour Office, 2001.

Periodicals

Louise Bernikow — "What Really Happened at Seneca Falls," *Ms.*, July/August 1998.

Alison Brower — "Glass Ceiling Survey," *Glamour*, April 2000.

Ellen Byron — "Girls, Interrupted," *Seventeen*, October 1999.

Melanie Conklin — "Blocking Women's Health Care: Your Hospital May Have a Policy You Don't Know About," *Progressive*, January 1998.

Mary H. Cooper — "Women and Human Rights," *CQ Researcher*, April 30, 1999.

CQ Researcher	"At Issue: Should the United States Ratify the Convention on the Elimination of All Forms of Discrimination Against Women?" April 30, 1999.
Donald DeMarco	"The Pill: From 'Freedom' to Fiasco," *Catholic Insight*, July 2000. Available from PO Box 625, Adelaide Station, 36 Adelaide St. East, Toronto, ON M5C 2J8 Canada.
Khadi Diallo	"Taking the Dress," *UNESCO Courier*, July 2001.
Christine Dinsmore	"Women's Health: A Casualty of Hospital Merger Mania," *Ms.*, July/August 1998.
Jennifer Erickson	"I'm Tired of Paying Big Bucks for Birth Control," *Self*, October 2000. Available from PO Box 55470, Boulder, CO 80322.
Susan R. Estrich	"Getting to the Top," *Working Woman*, September 2001.
Tom Fields-Meyer and Patrick Rogers	"Combat Zone: On the Sexual Battlefield, Women in the Military Find They Are Targets," *People Weekly*, May 5, 1997.
Nancy M. Fisher	"Gender Bias in Health Care," *Nurse Practitioner*, June 1997. Available from PO Box 90, 1111 Bethlehem Pike, Springhouse, PA 19477.
Sara Fisher and Elizabeth Hayes	"Unequal Under Law: Women Lawyers Still Scarce in Upper Ranks," *Los Angeles Business Journal*, February 9, 1998. Available from 5700 Wilshire Blvd., Suite 170, Los Angeles, CA 90036.
Olivia Gans and Mary Spaulding Balch	"Argument 2: A Woman Has the Right to Control Her Own Body," *National Right to Life News*, February 11, 1998. Available from 512 10th St. NW, Washington, DC 20004-1401.
Glamour	"Who's Trying to Block Your Access to Birth Control?" May 2001.
Anna Greenberg	"Will Choice Be Aborted?" *American Prospect*, September 24, 2001.
Robert J. Grossman	"It's Not Easy Being Green . . . and Female," *HR Magazine*, September 2001. Available from the Society for Human Resource Management, 1800 Duke St., Alexandria, VA 22314.
Stephanie Gutmann	"Sex and the Soldier: The Road from Aberdeen," *New Republic*, February 24, 1997.
Victor D. Infante	"Why Women Still Earn Less than Men," *Workforce*, April 2001. Available from 245 Fischer Ave. B-2, Costa Mesa, CA 92626.
Patricia Ireland	"Women's Rights," *Social Policy*, Spring 1998.
Leslie Laurence	"The Hidden Health Threat That Puts Every Woman at Risk," *Redbook*, July 2000.

Ruth F. Lax   "Socially Sanctioned Violence Against Women:
                                Female Genital Mutilation Is Its Most Brutal Form,"
                                Clinical Social Work Journal, Winter 2000.

Walter A. McDougall   "Sex, Lies, and Infantry," *Commentary*, September
                                1997.

Jill Nelson and   "Is Feminism a 4-Letter Word?" *Ms.*, February/March
Amy Aronson   2001.

New York Times   "Cracks in the Glass Ceiling," July 21, 1999.

Ursula A. O'Hare   "Realizing Human Rights for Women," *Human Rights
                                Quarterly*, May 1999.

Katha Pollitt   "Women's Rights: As the World Turns," *Nation*, March
                                29, 1999.

Susan E. Reed   "Taking the Bull by the Horns," *American Prospect*,
                                August 14, 2000.

Kit R. Roane and   "Afghan Women Find New Hope," *U.S. News & World
Ilana Ozernoy   Report*, December 3, 2001.

Maria Russo   "Your State, Your Rights: How Mandatory Counseling
                                and Waiting Periods Limit Your Access to Abortion,"
                                Self, May 1999.

Constance Rynder   "All Men and Women Are Created Equal," *American
                                History*, August 1998.

Joannie M. Schrof   "Feminism's Daughters: Their Agenda Is a Cultural Sea
                                Change," *U.S. News & World Report*, September 27,
                                1993.

Amartya Sen   "The Many Faces of Gender Inequality," *New Republic*,
                                September 17, 2001.

Deborah L. Shelton   "Not Just Little Men," *American Medical News*, May 5,
                                1997. Available from PO Box 109050, Chicago, IL
                                60610.

Annys Shin   "Reviving the ERA," *Ms.*, February/March 2000.

Andrew Sullivan   "RU4 Life," *New Republic*, October 16, 2000.

Joanne Symons   "Closing the Wage Gap Between Men and Women,"
                                Working Woman, January 2000.

Ann Scott Tyson   "Another Day, Another 75 Cents," *Christian Science
                                Monitor*, July 17, 1998.

Virginia Valian   "Running in Place," *The Sciences*, January/February
                                1998.

WIN News   "Women and Violence," Autumn 2001. Available
                                from Women's International Network, 187 Grant St.,
                                Lexington, MA 02420-2126.

Barry Yeoman   "The Quiet War on Abortion," *Mother Jones*,
                                September 2001.

Laura Ziv   "The Horror of Female Genital Mutilation: It's Been
                                Happening Here, and Now It's a Crime,"
                                Cosmopolitan, May 1997.

INDEX